# Praise for *Your Turn*

..................................................

"A well-told saga of recovery from loss and emotional breakdown, and a tribute to the ordinary blessings that made it possible."

**—KIRKUS REVIEWS**

"Telling stories and writing through your everyday stresses is the key takeaway in *Your Turn*. Dr. Tyra Manning believes that writing brings about clarity and hope in life. Her essential tools will help you get your inner thoughts onto paper and get you focused on the positives."

**—PARADE**

"Our worrisome thoughts can feel big, urgent, and uncontrollable. As Manning said, it can feel like we're 'getting caught in a whirlpool.' While we might not be drowning physically, we're drowning in negative chatter, she said. Even though our worries can feel overwhelming, we can shrink them. We can channel them into solutions—or we can reveal them for what they are: unhelpful, unreasonable, and illogical. The key is to know the difference."

**—PSYCH CENTRAL**

"*Your Turn* provides advice on composing even more precise, telling details that truly capture one's life journey, and for anyone wishing to tell her/his story, it's an unusually useful and specific handbook to guide one's writing."

**—COLEEN GRISSOM**, Ph. D Professor of English Trinity University

"*Your Turn*'s friendly and accessible tone makes it seem as if you're sitting down with a dear friend sharing stories over a cup of coffee, but Manning doesn't shy away from the hard realities of life's more challenging moments. The writing prompts and examples offer readers an opportunity to truly get to know themselves through their stories, and hers."

—**BRIDGET BOLAND**, Modern Muse

"Drawing on her own challenging life experiences, Dr. Tyra Manning presents an invitation and a guide to all of us to celebrate our lives through storytelling. As she remembered her own good times and bad times, she was rewarded with gifts of clarity, acceptance, forgiveness, and new perspectives on life. As you review your life experiences and share them with others, you reaffirm your own life—a task well worth pursuing."

—**W. WALTER MENNINGER**, M.D, psychiatrist of the Menninger Foundation, former dean of the Karl Menninger School of Psychiatry and Mental Health Science, former CEO of the Menninger Clinic, former editor of *Psychiatry Digest,* and nationally syndicated newspaper columnist

"Dr. Manning's book is a step-by-step roadmap to guide you through the maze that is writing your perfect memoir or autobiography. And the best part is that rather than reading like another 'how-to manual', *Your Turn* is filled with wonderful stories and anecdotes that give you a glimpse into the authors own life. It's a must read for any aspiring writer."

—**KAREN KEILT**, author of *The Parrot's Perch: A Memoir*

# Your Turn

## Ways to Celebrate Life Through Storytelling

## DR. TYRA MANNING

SHE WRITES PRESS

Published 2019
Printed in the United States of America
ISBN: 978-1-63152-456-1 pbk
ISBN: 978-1-63152-457-8 ebk
Library of Congress Control Number: 2019937621

For information, address:
She Writes Press
1569 Solano Ave #546
Berkeley, CA 94707
Credit: Where the Water Meets the Sand, by Tyra Manning was the original source of some of the material

Interior design by Tabitha Lahr

She Writes Press is a division of SparkPoint Studio, LLC.
All company and/or product names may be trade names, logos, trademarks, and/or registered trademarks and are the property of their respective owners.

Names and identifying characteristics have been changed to protect the privacy of certain individuals.

To all the storytellers and those who want to be. Tell your stories for yourself, those you love, and those you may never know. Write your stories and make a difference.

# Contents

# Introduction

..............................

Nothing helps us heal from the hurt feelings or resentments we bury deep in our hearts, from childhood through adulthood, like writing down our stories. I write about age-old pain left over from a quarrel with a sibling, an argument with my mother, or a bruise from a put-down on the playground that lives just below the surface of my skin, hidden, festering and gnawing at my psyche, a tattletale's admonition that I felt wronged and too frightened to stand up for myself. I write about residual grief from the loss of a relationship through death or the loss of a relationship due to a misunderstanding or the loss of a dear friend due to a physical move across the country. The kind of grief that weighs on my shoulders until even the smallest reminder that I can't have a cup of coffee with the person I'm missing overcomes me as I'm waiting at the Starbucks drive-thru window for my café breve latte while my favorite CD by Three Dog Night blares out "Joy to the World."

Writing my stories helps me remember the good times and the worst of times, and offers me the opportunity to understand them. Writing and celebrating my stories helps me heal. Hindsight gives me many gifts: clarity, acceptance, forgiveness, and new perspectives on past experiences. I'm not unique in having lovely and sometimes sad stories in my repertoire. Sharing our life stories teaches us that we have more commonalities than differences. It brings us closer together.

Sometimes, the most important stories are the ones that pop into our mind when we least expect them to. They are often spurred by seeing or doing something that reminds us of a particular event or person. I didn't intend to think about my grandfather PaPa, who grew watermelon in West Texas. But when I saw watermelon in the grocery store recently, it brought back memories of when I was a small child, searching with PaPa for the best watermelon in the patch.

"Okay, Tyra." He grinned as he broke the watermelon in half, plunged his huge hand into the center, and pulled out the sweet, dripping red heart.

"Sit here." He lifted me onto the bumper of his truck. "This is the best eatin' there is."

Music is also a strong catalyst for memory and writing. Music's rhythm helps me develop a cadence to my writing and helps me drown out unwanted thoughts. A few weeks after I checked myself into The Menninger Clinic, Mona, my sewing instructor, walked me over to the gymnasium for my first obligatory volleyball game. As we approached the gym, off in the distance I heard the familiar high-energy Three Dog Night rendition of their classic anthem "Joy to the World" blaring through the loudspeakers. A tiny shiver of happiness pulsed down my spine. I remember being surprised at the return of an emotion I hadn't felt since I'd fallen into a deep depression months earlier.

I walked tentatively into the gym, where other patients were lined up on opposing sides of the volleyball net, poised for the opening serve. Each team had some players who were clearly more swept away in the sheer joy of the musical moment than at the prospect of competing. Their bodies swayed back and forth to the beat of the song, caught up in their own expressions of exuberance and inspired to dance by the song and its nonsensical lyrics.

Lyle, our gym instructor, always started off our class with a short program of simple exercises. We seldom had enough players to field six players on each side of the net, but Lyle did his best to match the teams in a way that ensured equal competitiveness. The truth was that most of us were easily distracted and had a hard time staying focused on the game.

What I came to learn, however, was that volleyball was my time to physically move my body. Initially, the prospect of playing volleyball was depressing; I had never been a decent athlete. However, the experience became a form of respite for me from homesickness, from chronic worry about the well-being of my baby, Laura, and, most of all, from the all-consuming dread and fear I felt about the possibility that my husband, Larry, would be killed in the Vietnam War.

On good days, we fielded two teams of six players; other days, our teams were smaller, as some patients remained on the unit due to a "bad day." Fortunately, few of us cared about the outcome of the match. Instead, we embraced the absurdity of the moment, the silliness of the music, and the chance to be active as a group. It became a welcome break from the difficult emotional work we were doing.

"Joy to the World" remains one of my favorite songs. If no one else is around when I'm listening to it, I find myself sliding and twisting around, remembering with fondness my beautiful friends from the Clinic, and thinking about this strange, beautiful dance we call Life, for which there is no instruction manual, except for what's hidden within our hearts.

Favorite songs from my past revive memories that once were terribly sad but that now, thanks to the healing power of time, illuminate the touching and warm emotions those times evoked. When I write about experiences, both sad and happy, linked to important songs, those memories move from a place just under the surface of my skin and resurface in the present.

Writing my memoir, *Where the Water Meets the Sand*, was a bit like hiking through my own life's journey with a backpack of fresh hindsight mixed with poignant feelings from the past. Writing took me back to my childhood, but this time I was armed with the more mature and compassionate perspective of the woman I had grown into over the decades.

I hope this workbook encourages you to write and share your own stories. The chapters herein cover emotional themes ranging from grief, loss, and anger to joy, delight, and accomplishment. Each chapter ends with a section called "Your Turn," which is an invitation to write on three basic questions.

**What was it like at the beginning of the story?** Include the facts—where you were when the event took place, who was there, and how you felt.

**What happened?** Write the story like you would tell it verbally. Use active language and give examples. Include as much detail as possible to vividly recreate the scene. Most important, what was the issue? Was there a problem, a tragedy, a celebration?

**What was it like at the end of the story?** For me, the most important stories are those that teach us something. What did you learn from your experience? In writing *Where the Water Meets the Sand*, I realized that many of the lessons I learned in childhood, I later utilized and appreciated as an adult.

These prompts appear at the end of each chapter for easy reference. You can use them for anything that occurs in your life, even if it's not covered in one of the chapters in the workbook. As you write the facts and details of your stories, be sure to include how you felt, emotionally and physically. You may laugh out loud. Tears of happiness or sadness might well up in your eyes. Or you could feel a rash of chill bumps running down your arms. Whatever you feel, know that nothing is off-limits. Everything is fodder for the transformative power of your creativity.

# CHAPTER 1:

# Listening to Your Inner Voice

·····································································································

Since I was a small child, I've heard an inner voice. When I was young, that voice presented itself mostly in the form of intuitive surges of fear rather than as specific words. My father had a severe heart condition when I was a nine-year-old girl. When my parents traveled to doctors in search of a cure for Daddy's arteriosclerosis, I feared no one could help him.

One Sunday morning, I stayed home with Daddy while my mother and my brother went to church. Daddy and I were taking a nap when I awoke to him breathing heavily and gasping for breath. He reached for the small bottle of nitroglycerin pills on the nightstand. His face was pale, his lips bluish-purple. He was trying to tell me something, but he was gasping so hard I couldn't understand him. As he pointed at the pill bottle, I reached over to get one for him and accidentally spilled the precious medicine onto the floor. I retrieved the spilled pills from under the bed and I placed one under his tongue. After what seemed like forever, he began to breathe more slowly.

This story may not seem like a story of acting on intuition but one of being resourceful and taking action. But it was the fear, the strong and insistent feeling and recognition that something was very wrong, that stayed seared in my mind. The memory of Daddy's plight and his reliance on me that Sunday morning instilled in me the habit of respecting my inner fears and urgings. Paying attention to my inner voice, my intuition, became as natural as breathing.

Much later in my life, in 2007, I was feeling drained and exhausted. I couldn't shake the sense that something was wrong with me physically. I complained during an appointment with my internist that I felt weak all the time, like there was something wrong in my gut. He completed a routine examination and determined I was just fine.

When nothing changed over the next few weeks and I still didn't feel better, I called my doctor's office again. My fatigue was worse than before, and it wasn't easy to get to work on time.

At the end of my second appointment, he still couldn't find anything wrong with me. I told him I wanted a colonoscopy, but he was firm that there was no indication that I needed further testing. I wanted him to be correct and left determined to buck up and do my best. Yet I still worried about it. As an educator I owed my students my best efforts, but I was exhausted and struggling.

One Sunday afternoon my daughter, Laura, and my nephew were in my kitchen, preparing Sunday lunch. I walked outside to admire my newly manicured yard and thanked God for the beautiful day with my family.

My inner voice responded, *Too bad you're not going to live long enough to enjoy it.*

I immediately called my internist at home and insisted, "I want a colonoscopy and I want it now."

When the doctor called with the results, he said, "Tyra, I am so sorry. You have cancer."

Some of my colon had to be removed, and I began chemotherapy. In some ways, I was relieved. I'd known something was wrong. I am forever grateful that I listened to my inner voice. Had I ignored it, things might have turned out much differently. I'm often asked, "But how did you know to follow through?" I knew because I didn't feel well. I intuitively knew something was terribly wrong.

# YOUR TURN

..........................................................

We all have an inner voice, an intuitive guidance system that is ready to give us information anytime we need it. Write about a time in your life when your intuition had information for you. Use these guidelines to tell your story.

**What was it like at the beginning of the story?** Include the facts—where you were, when the event took place, who was there, and how you felt.

**What happened?** Write the story like you would tell it verbally. Use active language and give examples. Include as much detail as possible to vividly recreate the scene. Most important, what was the issue? Was there a problem, a tragedy, a celebration?

**What was it like at the end of the story?** For me, the most important stories are those that teach us something. What did you learn from your experience? In writing *Where the Water Meets the Sand*, I realized that many of the lessons I learned from my childhood, I later utilized and appreciated as an adult.

# CHAPTER 2:

# Love and Larry

..............................................

One of the brightest times in my life was when I met Larry Hull on a blind date my freshman year at Texas Tech in Lubbock, Texas. It was September 1965. My roommate Gina and her fiancé, Ronnie, introduced me to Larry. Ronnie lived across the hall from Larry in one of the men's dorms on campus. Ronnie had introduced Gina to Larry, and she told me Larry was twenty years old, a handsome blue-eyed blond sophomore, and the son of an air force sergeant whose family had lived overseas in Japan. She explained that Larry's dad was temporarily stationed in Guam while Larry's mother and younger brother lived on the air force base in Roswell, New Mexico.

"Larry is close to his family and goes home to Roswell to be with his mother while his dad is out of the country as often as he can," she said. "He works at the Base Exchange on the weekends when he goes home to help out with his college expenses." Both Gina and Ronnie were impressed with Larry and thought he would be a suitable match for me.

The first thought I had when Larry picked me up in his 1957 Chevy was that my father would have approved. Daddy had been the manager and junior partner of a Chevrolet, Oldsmobile, and Buick dealership in Seminole, Texas, before he died of heart failure when I was nine years old.

Daddy always said, "The way a man keeps his car tells you a lot about his character. If he keeps it clean and in order, he is proud. He's a man who cares about how he presents himself."

Daddy kept his car waxed so that your reflection stared back at you when you stood next to it. He drove his cars with confidence and grace. The appearance of Daddy's cars matched his dress. He always wore white starched shirts, shiny cuff links, a necktie, and a dark suit.

Larry reminded me of Daddy, proud, masculine, yet graceful, all in one neat gentlemanly package. The chrome on Larry's two-tone lavender-and-white '57 Belair Chevy sparkled and the shimmery black metallic upholstery was immaculate. Larry smiled as he opened the passenger side door for me. Before he started the engine, his first words were, "Are you comfortable?" After he settled into the driver's seat, he told me where he planned to take me. "We're going to Reese Air Force Base to watch the planes take off. I never get tired of watching the landing patterns.

"One day I'm going to officer's training school and become a pilot," Larry announced. "I've wanted to be a pilot since I was a little boy. Dad always took our family to the air shows on the base and taught me the names of the planes and what they were used for. I've spent lots of hours since I was little at the flight line watching the planes take off." Larry's eyes sparkled when he talked about his plans.

"I've never flown anywhere," I replied, "but it sounds exciting."

"My dad and I used to play a game," Larry went on. "I had to name each plane and tell its purpose in the air force. He not only taught me the names of the planes but explained why each one was necessary."

Goosebumps ran down my spine. Larry not only loved his dad, he was proud of him.

"My dad is Chief Master Sergeant Robert Hull," Larry said. "Men like him keep the planes flying and in tip-top shape."

Then he added, "Tell me about your family. What does your dad do?"

Tears welled as I told Larry about Daddy and his fatal heart attack. Larry's life was so different from mine. He put his arm around my shoulders as if he understood my heartache. Feeling reassured, I went on to tell him that I was third-generation Texan, and most of my relatives lived within a hundred-mile radius of Seminole, Texas, where I grew up.

"Really?" Larry seemed pleased. "Sounds like my mother's family in Alabama. They all live in the Mobile Bay area. My maternal grandmother, Mama, and granddaddy, Pop, live in the hills outside of Citronelle, a small town near Mobile. Uncle Orrin is the Pentecostal preacher on weekends at a church not far from Mama and Pop. His family lives outside of Mobile where he works in a lumberyard during the week. My uncle Sonny and my mother's sister and her family live there too," Larry said.

" I have an Uncle Sonny too!" I exclaimed. "He's a very successful farmer, but his love is training horses. All of my grandparents were farmers in West Texas."

"Mama and Pop raised me while my mother worked in a canning factory in Mobile. Mother came to Citronelle on the weekends," Larry continued.

Although our lives seemed very different on the surface, our grandparents were country people and each of our extended families lived within a hundred-mile radius of one another.

Larry went on. "If Mom hadn't married my dad and he hadn't adopted me when I was three years old, I'd probably be working in the lumber mills or on an oil rig off the Gulf Coast. One of my cousins, about my age, worked on an oil rig in the Gulf—"

"Really? My uncle Rusty is a tool pusher on oil rigs in New Mexico," I chimed in.

Larry pointed to a plane above our heads coming in on its approach for landing. Its engines roared so loud we couldn't hear one another. "That's gonna be me someday in the cockpit.

"What about you?" he asked. "What do you want to do when you finish school?"

"I want to be a teacher like my mother. Maybe even a principal," I added.

"There are schools on air force bases," Larry said. "When your family's in the service, you can travel around the world and still be able to follow your dreams."

I felt as if Larry were a recruitment officer for the air force. I had just met him, yet it felt as if I had known him before, and we seemed to be weaving a story of possibilities together.

"Are you hungry? Pops makes the best spaghetti," Larry promised. I nodded and we headed back to Lubbock where Larry slid his lavender Chevy into the crowded parking space in front of Pops'.

The minute Larry opened the door and we sat down at a plastic red-and-white tablecloth, Pops appeared at our table.

"Who's your friend?" Pops asked as he poked Larry on the shoulder.

Larry grinned. "Somebody you're going to like, Pops."

While we ate, Larry wanted to hear more about Daddy, Mother, and my sister and brother. It was as if we both couldn't stop asking questions about each other. We wanted to know as much as we could about the other as fast as we could, as if we were trying to make up for a lifetime of not knowing one another.

*I know you*, I thought. *I know what it's like to have a dream.*

Soon Pops was whispering, "Hey guys, I've got to close."

The electric energy between beautiful blue-eyed blond Larry Hull and me felt tangible. When Larry walked me to the door of my residence, his arm locked with mine. He stared straight into my eyes and asked, "May I call you tomorrow?" I nodded yes, and he squeezed my hand.

After that, we were together whenever possible. We attended classes at Texas Tech, studied together, and planned our future as if being together was ordained by the universe.

My mother, however, was not sold on the idea. When I announced to her that Larry's mother had invited me to spend Thanksgiving in Roswell with his family, Mother made her reservations known. "Who is this boy, and why would you miss Thanksgiving with your family to spend the holiday with someone you just met?"

Though her displeasure stung, I had heard Mother tell stories about her admiration and connection with my father from the time he enrolled in the country school she attended when she was in third grade. I tried to make her understand that I felt the same immediate bond with Larry: "He's special. I enjoy being with him and feel a strong connection with him. He's a gentleman around me, not like the other boys our age. I look forward to spending time with him.

"I'm going," I told her. Mother pouted and showed her disapproval by barely speaking to me before I left for Thanksgiving with Larry's family. The distance between us expanded until the day I left for New Mexico and Larry's house.

When I pulled up to the gate of the air force base in Roswell, Larry and his lavender Chevy were waiting on the other side of the gate. As the guard motioned me forward, I felt a heavy knot in my throat. The flags and the MPs filled me with awe and a mixture of fear and excitement. I admired men and women who served our country. My father had been in the service, and my grandfather had fought in France in WWI. Uncle Frank, my daddy's older brother, was overseas in WWII.

When the guard waved me through the gate, it was as if the road to my life opened ahead of me. We were on that road, Larry and me and the United States Air Force. It was a dream worth fighting for.

Mrs. Hull's hair was blond like Larry's. Her smile was contagious and telegraphed a genuine graciousness similar to Larry's demeanor. She hugged me tight and immediately began a nonstop list of the foods she had prepared. "Larry wrote a list of some of your favorite foods: I have celery filled with cream cheese and chives, pumpkin pie with whipped cream, and hot, strong coffee. Are you hungry after your drive? Sit down here. I'll put snacks on the table while we visit. The turkey will be ready soon. We're so excited you're here."

Larry and his mother began working in the kitchen while I sat at the table snacking on green onion dip and potato chips, answering the plethora of questions Mrs. Hull directed my way.

"Mom, not so many questions all at once," Larry cautioned. "She just got here."

"It's no problem," I assured them both. "Larry, I love that your mom is so interested in getting to know about me and my family. The two of us have spent a good amount of time getting to know each other and about each other's families. Why wouldn't your mom want to do the same?" *This family is so easy and comfortable to be around*, I thought.

After dinner, Larry and Mrs. Hull washed dishes while I sat at the table and heard stories about their family living in Japan when PaPa Hull was stationed at Walker Air Force Base, and about his mother's family in Alabama.

Mrs. Hull said, "When you meet my relatives, they'll treat you like family. That's because you're with Larry, and they all just love Larry."

*Who doesn't love Larry?* I wondered. I couldn't remember feeling so much at home in a long time.

The next morning, as soon as we'd finished breakfast and the dishes were washed and dried, Larry insisted on giving me a tour of the base. We got in Larry's car. Before we backed out of the carport, Larry said, "It's so good to have you here with me and my family for Thanksgiving. Mother is so excited and thrilled to meet you."

First we went to the flight line to see the planes. Larry's love for planes seemed to have no end. I listened carefully as he named each plane assigned to the Walker Air Force Base. He pointed out the air traffic control tower and all the other important aspects of the air force base. I nodded and acted interested because Larry loved the base, the planes, and showing them off. I had no experience with air force bases, though I wanted to learn because it was important to Larry. Much of what he told me went over my head, but it didn't matter. I loved his excitement, his determination to live his dream and be a pilot, and I loved him. I loved that he had a dream. I knew he would fulfill it. I wanted to be a part of that dream.

When the weekend was over, Larry and I returned to Lubbock for semester finals. Christmas was barely four weeks away. It would be our first. I had not enjoyed Christmas since Daddy died, but now I was convinced the holidays would be fantastic because I had Larry.

Rather than drive directly to Roswell for Christmas with his mom and younger brother, Larry followed me in his car from Lubbock to my grandmother's for Christmas with my extended family on Mother's side. I was worried my uncles would give him a hard time—my uncles were such teases and this was the first special date I had invited to meet the family. One of my uncles, Kurtis, my mother's youngest brother, was a real pistol when it came to his nieces' young suitors. After Daddy died, he was especially protective of me.

Fortunately, even though his life was very different from my relatives, Larry was a hit with them. He didn't take teasing personally and was good at giving it back without being rude—as evidenced by something that happened right before Larry left to go to Roswell to be with his mother and his younger brother for Christmas.

We decided to take a drive around the farm in his car. We parked not far from the farmhouse and walked through the pasture.

"I wish we could be together for Christmas," I whined.

"We'll have lots of Christmases together," he consoled me, "but it's important that we honor our families during the holidays, especially with Dad overseas. Besides, since you spent Thanksgiving with me and my family, it's only right that you're with your folks for Christmas."

All of a sudden, a long-eared jackrabbit popped out from behind an old broken-down trailer. He was out of sight in seconds as he disappeared over the draw.

"So that's a jackalope," Larry exclaimed, grinning from ear to ear. "When we go back to the house, I'm ready to spin a tall tale for your uncle Kurtis."

Sure enough, the minute we walked in after our walk, Uncle Kurtis began his teasing. "So what'd you learn on your walk? Anything jump out at you?"

Larry leaned back, each hand pushed down into his Levi's pockets, and egged Uncle Kurtis on. "I was disappointed, to be honest. I was hoping to see a jackalope. I understood they were humongous in Texas. As Tyra and I walked down through the draw by that rickety, broken-down trailer down there, all we saw was one jackrabbit jump out from behind the trailer. I'm really disappointed," Larry moaned. "His antlers were barely little ol' stumps growing out of his head, and he was puny. Really puny." Larry wouldn't quit. "Seriously, the poor thing was a sad sight to see—just plain pitiful."

Uncle Kurtis's face turned beet red. He knew he'd been outdone and one-upped by Larry, so he stood up and gave Larry a sincere handshake. Then he grabbed Larry and gave him a manly hug. From then on, they remained close.

———

After Larry returned to his family, those days apart felt like forever. We were both elated to be back at school together after the holiday.

One night before spring registration, we were poring over the class schedule at Pops'. Pops came over to our table ceremoniously carrying a warmed brownie à la mode topped with an unlit gold candle. Grinning from ear to ear, Pops placed it in front of me. Even though Larry acted surprised, I could tell he was pretending. Larry reached across the table and took my hand. Our knees were pressed together under the table.

"I know this is soon, but I love you so much. Will you marry me?" he asked softly.

"Yes," I said before he could finish. Larry lit the candle and lifted me from my chair in a huge bear hug. We set our wedding date for as soon as the spring semester ended.

As sure as I was that I wanted to spend the rest of my life with Larry, something was weighing on me. I had to share it with him to make sure that it wouldn't change his decision.

When Larry took me home that night, before we got out of his car, I said, "There's something I need to tell you. Two years ago we were living in Abilene during the summer so Mother could take classes for her master's degree at Abilene Christian College. Even though in my heart I knew I was pregnant, I couldn't face the reality in my mind. I finally saw a doctor in secret. He confirmed that I was pregnant.

"I didn't want to cause Mother any more trouble, since I had been a difficult teenager. After Daddy died, I told her I was going to the high school library to study on weeknights. Rather than go to the library, I went to Hobbs, New Mexico, to buy beer. I drank in secret. I also frequently met a boy who was special to me and with whom I went parking. He was the father of my baby.

"Unfortunately, my grades plummeted my junior year. The last thing Mother needed to hear was that I was pregnant, so I didn't tell her about the baby until I found a place in Abilene where I could live, sponsored by a local church, until my baby was born.

"As the summer drew to an end, we were planning on going home to Seminole, I finally told my mother.

"She was upset, stressed, and worried. I assured her I would be fine. She and my sister went home for the new school year—Mother was a teacher and needed to go to work—while I stayed in Abilene. My baby girl was born on October 5, 1964. I kept it a secret from my friends and told them I had decided to finish the fall semester at Cooper High School. The truth is, I took my classes from a private tutor.

"I almost died from eclampsia after going into convulsions. Thank God, the baby lived, and so did I. When the spring semester began, I moved home to Seminole and graduated with my high school class.

"Maybe you won't want to marry me now," I whispered.

Tears filled Larry's eyes as he pulled me to his chest. "Tyra, my daddy adopted me when he married my mother. I was three years old. If it hadn't been for my dad, I would be working in the lumber mills in Alabama. I love you." At that moment, I knew I belonged with Larry Hull forever. That night, when Larry walked me to my door, he said, "Tyra, maybe I love you even more after what you shared with me tonight."

Now that Larry knew my secret, the heaviness in my heart began to evaporate. Larry's response set me free. The fear that he wouldn't want to marry me after the news of my teenage pregnancy vanished.

Larry's mother was thrilled about our engagement. My mother's reaction was a different story. She was disappointed in me and didn't want to discuss our wedding plans with us.

Larry suggested we invite her for coffee at a local restaurant before she left for Seminole, our hometown. Mother was already waiting for us in a booth when we arrived at the restaurant. There were no congratulations from Mother. I hadn't expected any. I had avoided her after her reaction to our engagement. My body stiffened as I scooted into the booth facing her. After a time that seemed to go on forever, she turned and spoke to Larry as if I wasn't there.

"How are you going to support my daughter?" she demanded.

Larry tried to reassure her and made it clear we would both graduate from college. "Mrs. Decker, we'll get by." His voice was kind and confident.

I cringed as I listened to Mother's response. "I didn't raise Tyra to just 'get by.' She deserves better."

I wanted to crawl under the table. I wanted to grab Larry's hand and stomp out of the restaurant.

I'll never forget Larry's response. "Mrs. Decker, I love your daughter," he told her. "I'll always care for her. We have dreams and promises to one another that we'll each keep. I'll always love her, and she feels the same about me. I'm committed to changing your mind about me and our marriage."

As rude and hateful as I thought Mother was acting, I recognized at the same time that she had been widowed when I was nine, my brother was fourteen, and she was pregnant with our new baby. Larry encouraged me to give Mother time and to try to understand her perspective and that she wanted what was best for me. His confidence in standing up to her on our behalf without one shred of rudeness amazed me then and still does.

Soon after we were engaged, my maternal grandmother, Nennie, came to Lubbock to take Larry and me to lunch at Furr's cafeteria. Nennie and Larry had been close from the time they met one another. She asked if we had our hearts set on wedding rings and explained that the jeweler in Brownfield, her hometown, was a client of hers. She was sure he would give us a great price on any matching sets of rings we chose. We were thrilled and drove to Brownfield one Saturday morning not long after to pick out our rings at Connor's Jewelry.

"Are you interested in plain bands or diamonds?" the proprietor, Mr. Connor, inquired soon after we arrived. Larry was committed to a wedding set that included an engagement ring. It seemed like Mr. Connor brought out over half of his merchandise before we had an idea of our choices and the rings we really liked. After trying on set after set for at least two or three hours, we selected a set—an engagement ring with a solitaire mounted on a wide band that matched wide wedding bands adorned with diamond chips for each of us. I'll never forget the tears of joy that welled up in Larry's eyes once we decided on our magnificent choices.

Uncle Kurtis and Aunt Laurel invited everyone, including Mother, over for a celebratory lunch. Most everyone oohed and aahed over my engagement ring—except for my mom. My joy that day dimmed a bit at Mother's reaction, though I wasn't surprised. She had made her feelings known.

I was vindicated six months later when Mother told Larry and me how wrong she had been about him and our marriage. She told both of us he was a son-in-law who would make any mother-in-law proud. When Mother apologized, Larry hugged her and said, "Mrs. Decker, you were only wanting the best for Tyra. I love being a part of this family." Mother's eyes filled with tears, as did mine.

We set the wedding date for May 28, 1966, and the next few months flew by.

Nennie came back to Lubbock on business and told us over lunch at Furr's that she had a surprise for me. She drove me to Margaret's, one of the nicest dress shops in Lubbock. Margaret and Nennie were friends. When we arrived, it was clear Margaret was expecting us. The three of us picked out a gorgeous mantilla veil for my wedding. Mother was making my wedding dress, and Nennie said the mantilla veil would set the standard.

Mother did make a gorgeous wedding gown. The long sleeves and tailored full-length sheath with a wide lace trim from the neck to the hem of the dress fit beautifully. The mantilla veil that trailed below my waist was elegant.

Holding our wedding and reception at the First Baptist Church I attended as a child made it so special for me and my family. The church was filled with relatives, family friends, and precious friends from high school. Larry was handsome, wearing a white formal jacket and black trousers with black stripes down the sides. White and yellow daisies covered the wedding arch and filled a large bouquet I carried. My brother, Rodney, gave me away. Larry's dad was out of the country on temporary duty, but his mother and young brother, Albert, were welcomed by my relatives and friends. My grandmother Nennie and my father's mother, Maw Maw, were alive and both healthy enough to attend. Larry's friends from high school and fraternity brothers also attended.

After the reception, we headed off on our honeymoon at a ski resort in Ruidoso, New Mexico. It was May and there was no snow, but the resort was beautiful. We rode the ski lift to observe the mountains from a different perspective. We had enough money to spend two nights at the resort and stopped by Larry's family's home and spent the night with Larry's mother and Albert on the base in Roswell on our way back from our honeymoon. We had very little money, but we were elated and in love. That was all that mattered.

We moved into married couples' apartments for Texas Tech students and began searching for jobs. Larry worked full-time as a stock boy at Southwestern Bell Telephone Company where he was promoted to work the night shift resetting the reel-to-reel data tapes in the computer room. He continued to carry a full load of university classes. I was hired as a part-time medical records clerk at Methodist Hospital and also attended classes part-time at Texas Tech. It was a marvelous time to be young. We thought we were the luckiest couple we knew. We had jobs, and were both determined to graduate from the university. Larry was enrolled in a bachelor's program in business administration, and I was enrolled in the school of education. We were on our way to living our dream.

Larry graduated in 1968 with a bachelor's degree in business. Larry had promised we'd take a vacation to Alabama after his graduation so that I could meet his grandparents and other relatives. I had heard so much about his grandmother, Mama, and his grandfather, Pop, I couldn't wait.

The vacation came at just the right time. In addition to graduating, Larry had been accepted by the USAF for Officer Training School (OTS) and would receive his second lieutenant commission. After our vacation, Larry would begin pilot training back in Lubbock, Texas. His lifelong dream to be an officer and a pilot was set in motion.

We had also just learned I was pregnant. We were both thrilled, though I privately worried about Larry's potential deployment once he completed pilot training. Deployment to Vietnam would most likely be next. With Larry by my side, I couldn't dwell on his potential deployment too much. One of the loveliest things about Larry was his unmasked excitement and unadulterated joy. When I raised concerns or verbalized anxiety, he'd say something like, "It will work out, Tyra. Don't worry. It'll all work out." As long as I was with him, I believed him.

Despite my worries, I couldn't wait for our trip to Alabama. Larry had told me we would walk in the woods, pick wild plums, and see where so many of the stories he had told me had taken place. The icing on the cake was scheduled for the end of our trip. Larry had promised to take me crabbing at Mobile Bay.

Larry's stories about his childhood were filled with rich details. But it was Larry's dad's tale of meeting Larry for the first time that amazed me the most. After Mrs. Hull married Larry's adoptive father, Master Sergeant Robert J. Hull, she took him to meet Larry outside Citronelle where Larry lived with his maternal grandparents.

Larry's dad, Papa Hull, described the story of his first meeting with Larry: "He was only three years old, stripped down to his birthday suit with shoulder-length blond curly hair. When Mama called Larry to lunch, he peeked out from behind a tall tree behind Mama and Pop's tiny house.

"Larry must have seen us drive up," Papa Hull surmised, "and he was deciding whether or not to come in for lunch. It took some coaxing, but he couldn't resist seeing his mother."

That was my favorite story about Larry that I learned in Alabama. He tolerated hearing it but turned bright red every time one of the relatives would begin to tell it. I thought it was precious, although the idea that Larry had roamed the woods in the nude at three years old in Alabama was hard to imagine, given that he had grown into a fastidious, hyper-neat, soon-to-be USAF officer. The more I learned about Larry Hull, the more I loved him.

We returned to Lubbock after our trip to Alabama. Soon after Larry was inducted into the air force, he deployed to San Antonio for Officer Training School. I remained at Texas Tech to continue my degree in education. Larry earned his second lieutenant bars and was assigned to Reese Air Force Base for pilot training, where our baby girl, Laura Elizabeth, was born March 4, 1969. After a year of pilot training, Larry earned his wings and was deployed to Fort Walton Beach in Florida for pilot training on a forward air controller, the plane he would fly in Vietnam. The thought of losing Larry like I had lost my dad turned into a nightmare.

After Larry left for Florida, I was overwhelmed and I couldn't concentrate on my college classes. During a regular appointment with my gynecologist, I told him how distressed and fearful I was. Dr. Doran recommended I see a colleague of his, a psychiatrist from New York. After three sessions with the psychiatrist, he diagnosed me with clinical depression. He recommended psychiatric hospitalization at Methodist Hospital. After two hospitalizations at Methodist, he said, "Go to Florida and be with your husband. It's important that you and your family have this time together before Larry is deployed to Vietnam." That was all Larry and I needed. I would return to school after Larry went to Vietnam.

Larry and I were thrilled that we would be together in Florida. He rented a mobile home on the bay side of the Gulf. My fears eased as we built bonfires and boiled shrimp on the beach with the other pilots and their wives. Laura and I built castles in the sand during the day while Larry trained on the plane he would fly in Vietnam. At night, after Laura was in bed, Larry and I sat on the pier, trailing our feet over the tops of the waves splashing below. As we watched the sun dip below the horizon, he'd slip his arm around my waist and nestle close to me.

"When I'm gone and you're lonely and miss me, look up at the sky and think of me. On the other side of the world, I'll look up at the very same stars and moon and think of you and Laura," he whispered in my ear. The night sky over the water was spectacular. It reminded me of the wide skies of West Texas. But memories of unanswered prayers to those same heavens as a child spoiled my sense of peace.

Training on the forward air controller flew by quickly and Larry's dream to fly for the USAF became a reality while I lived in terror that my nightmare of losing Larry was coming true. After he completed training in Florida, we moved back to Lubbock, moved out of base housing, and bought a new trailer house for Laura and me just weeks before Larry deployed.

"If something happens to me, you and Laura will own a place of your own," he said. I appreciated his proactive planning but viewed his purchase of the trailer house as a bad omen.

The day Larry deployed for Vietnam, he awoke excited. "Today's the day," he exclaimed. We had been counting down the days before he deployed. He'd counted them down with excitement. His lifelong dream of being an air force pilot was becoming a reality. I counted down the days to his departure with dread and fear—fear that I would lose the love of my life like I had lost my father when I was nine.

Larry showered while I dressed and chose Laura's cutest outfit, a blue-and-white checked dress with matching panties. Larry was handsome in his dress blues, his silver wings pinned above his pocket. Larry drove to the airport with Laura standing between the two of us. The cloudy skies and rain matched my mood. I didn't dare let Larry know how much his leaving devastated me. A scene from a movie the two of us had watched on our black-and-white television set flashed through my mind. When a young pilot in the movie was killed, Larry had said, "If I don't come home from Vietnam, I want to be buried at Arlington."

"I promise," I had assured him, not understanding the uncertainty of keeping promises in wartime.

As soon as Larry pulled our white Chevrolet Impala into the airport parking lot, I got out of the passenger seat, lifted the baby from the front seat, and walked around to the driver's side.

"Don't come inside with me," he insisted as he gathered the two of us in his arms. "You are my beautiful girls."

A broad smile spread across his face, telegraphing his excitement that his dream of being an air force pilot and serving his country was coming true. He retrieved two photos from his wallet. "These are my two favorite girls. I'll keep them with me always. Honey, be sure to show Laura my picture every day. Tell her, 'This is your Daddy who loves you very much.'"

He turned to Laura. "Be sweet, eat good so you'll be strong, and do what Mommy asks. Daddy loves you."

Laura twisted around to stare at the tears rolling down my face as Larry reached over and wiped them away. He reminded me that in case of emergencies, I had money in our savings account. He assured me he had faith in me and before we knew it, it would be time for R&R in Hawaii.

He slid Laura to his left hip so he could kiss me good-bye and pulled me to his chest. It was like all of our kisses but longer than usual. His eyes watered as he traced the outline of my lips. I stepped back so he could be with Laura. He held her out in front of him, then kissed her forehead and cheeks. "I love you. Now go to Mommy," he cooed as he handed her to me.

"Good-bye. I'll always love my girls. Don't look back. The next time you see me, I'll be home."

I followed Larry's advice and did not watch him leave, as if following his instructions would ensure his safe return.

# YOUR TURN

........................................

Write about a great love in your own life. You may love a spouse, partner, child, parent, grandparent, lifelong friend, pet, or even a thing. Some people, especially those who make a commitment to God through the clergy or through missionary work, may choose to write about that kind of love. There is no judgment here; just write your truth.

**What was it like at the beginning of the story?** Include the facts—where you were, when the event took place, who was there, and how you felt.

**What happened?** Write the story like you would tell it verbally. Use active language and give examples. Include as much detail as possible to vividly recreate the scene. Most important, what was the issue? Was there a problem, a tragedy, a celebration?

**What was it like at the end of the story?** For me, the most important stories are those that teach us something. What did you learn from your experience? In writing *Where the Water Meets the Sand*, I realized that many of the lessons I learned in childhood, I later utilized and appreciated as an adult.

# CHAPTER 3:

# Just Lock Me Up

........................................................

The same awful day Larry left for Nam, I drove Laura from the airport to the babysitter's and then drove home to the trailer house Larry had bought for us just days before he left. I needed time to pull myself together after watching Larry's plane take off. I was fearful my tears would worry the baby.

As soon as I arrived at the house, I hurried inside and moved straight to the bathroom. I reached for the "tools" I kept hidden under my sink in our bathroom. I had toyed with cutting by making halfhearted scratches on my wrist as Larry's deployment date grew closer. Like a surgeon setting out her instruments, I neatly arranged a double-edged razor blade, washcloth, cotton balls, a bottle of rubbing alcohol, and a container of Band-Aids on the bathroom counter. Kneeling before the toilet, my left arm supported by the toilet seat, I hung my left wrist over the toilet bowl and went to work.

The first cut was ineffective because I was timid. I grew braver as I worked. The third cut was deep. Blood gushed from my wrist. I held my arm over the toilet and watched as the blood ran into the bowl, dissolving from bright red to pink like cherry Kool-Aid in a pitcher of water. Hypnotized by the swirling pink clouds as I rested my head on the toilet seat, I no longer felt panicked or crazy. Tranquility washed over me. Peace, just like "the peace that passeth all understanding" from the scriptures the preacher read when I was a child.

I realized I needed to go to the emergency room. No explanation made sense. I told the admitting nurse that I'd cut myself and needed help. The nurse scowled and walked me into an examination room. After I received several stitches, I hurried out the door, humiliated and overwhelmed.

As a troubled teenager, I'd begun bingeing and purging. It was an accidental discovery. I wanted to be thin, popular, and attractive. It was about the same time I began sneaking beer from a friend's parents. I thought I was overweight and ugly, and I dieted frequently. The first time I binged and purged was after I had starved myself so I could fit into a new outfit that was too small for me. I was amazed that I could eat anything I wanted, purge, and not gain weight. When I first started, it was not an ongoing habit. Through the summer between my freshman and sophomore year, I used both as coping skills. Bingeing and purging calmed my anxiety. I didn't understand why I was so anxious. I missed my dad who had died when I was nine, and though I was smart, I was obstinate. Unfortunately, and much to my relief at the time, I had discovered what I learned years later was a disease called bulimia. At the time, I perceived it as a method of controlling my weight and an antidote for anxiety.

I'd never heard about anyone cutting deliberately, but something inside me instinctively believed that if I could bleed out the bad feelings, I might get better. Once Larry was gone, I cut more and more frequently, needing to draw blood. As my emotional state grew more precarious, I seldom prepared for class assignments and left Laura at the sitter's for longer periods than my schedule required in case I needed to cut.

I was seeing my psychiatrist once a week, even though I didn't tell him about my secret coping tricks. I did tell him that I was depressed and could barely get out of bed, that I felt unable to care for Laura or keep up with my studies. He recommended

I be admitted to the psychiatric ward at Methodist Hospital again. I'd been there for nearly six weeks when my psychiatrist suggested that I go to The Menninger Clinic in Topeka, Kansas, for treatment. Menninger was one of the best mental hospitals in the country, and the air force would pay for it. My psychiatrist believed I could get well faster with long-term inpatient care. I agreed. I was getting worse. I made deeper cuts on my wrists. When I dreamt of Larry's plane crashing, I binged on mounds of food and then vomited. Exhausted and feeling as if there was no escape from terrible days of self-punishment, I slept for hours. I was afraid—afraid that I couldn't take care of Laura as she deserved, and I was afraid for myself. Each day, I felt only disgust and loathing. It was as if I lived in hell and something within me was intent on keeping me there. I felt guilty over not living up to my promises to take care of Laura and stay in school. I heaped self-loathing and vengeance on my soul and I couldn't quit. It was as if I didn't punish me, the devil would.

Sometimes these behaviors released the pressure of the feelings building inside and gave me the energy to read Laura a story or give her a bath. Other times, cutting or gorging and vomiting were like drugs or alcohol. Afterward I slept for hours. I was afraid for Laura to be alone with me. I wasn't afraid of what I might do; I was afraid of what I might forget: I might forget to feed her, or fall asleep and leave her alone too long.

By the time the psychiatrist suggested inpatient care, I was desperate to get better. But I had to wait for an opening at Menninger. I grew so despondent that I had to go live with my mother in Seminole. I could no longer take care of myself, let alone a toddler. Mother had a full-time teaching job, so Laura stayed in Lubbock with her babysitter Janelle and her family.

Being separated from my daughter was even more excruciating than being apart from Larry. I feared that Laura would feel as abandoned as I had when Mother and Daddy traveled to find doctors to help my father, but I had no choice. There were days I couldn't get out of bed except to go to the bathroom.

Mother tried to help me as best she could. In the mornings, she left me in bed while she went to work. When she came home for lunch at noon, I was still there. She coaxed me into getting up and having lunch with her, and then went back to work.

I stayed in bed most of the day, except for making secret runs to the Dairy Queen to buy mountains of hamburgers, French fries, and ice cream. I consumed the food, purged, and then hid back under the covers. Like cutting, though not as effective, gorging and vomiting relieved my escalating anxiety and the sense that all the fear building up inside of me was about to blow off the top of my head. It kept me going during the four weeks I waited for a room to become available at Menninger.

Monday through Friday, I called the Menninger social worker assigned to my case, Nolan Brohaugh, in the hopes that someone had been discharged, even though I had been told the wait time was approximately five weeks. I also called a friend of my grandmother's. She was the only person I knew who had been a patient at the Clinic, and I needed to hear her tell me over and over that Menninger was a good hospital and could help me. Some days I wondered whether going to The Menninger Clinic was a good idea, until one day, after a hamburger bingeing spree at the Dairy Queen, the necessary purging ritual, and the long nap that usually followed, I dreamt about Uncle Sonny and learning to ride Old Sox, one of the horses at my grandparents' farm.

Uncle Sonny was the epitome of a southern cowboy. Late in his teens, he left home to ride the rodeo circuit and only returned after he'd broken both legs. Folks said he could tame any horse he met. He was a true horse whisperer, and the gentlest, kindest man I knew as a child. I'm sure the horses could sense it, too.

Mother always said my grandfather PaPa had no use for horses. He said they ate tons of food and didn't pull their weight on the farm. He was terribly disappointed when his son left the farm for such foolishness.

One summer while I was visiting Nennie and PaPa at their farm, Sonny was out working with some of the horses he boarded there. I was barely a teenager and, frankly, afraid of horses. I wandered down to the corral where Sonny was working.

"Uncle Sonny," I said, "could you teach me to ride? I'm afraid of horses but I'd like to learn."

"Well, that's a problem," Uncle Sonny said. "You can't show your fear. Horses can smell fear and they'll take you for a ride for sure. I'll hoist you up into the saddle and walk you around the corral. That's all we'll do the first time. All you have to do is sit easy in the saddle and relax," he assured me as he held the stirrup steady for my left foot while I mounted and swung my right leg over.

Steadying myself in the saddle, I pushed my right foot into the stirrup. The sides of the horse were huge. As Old Sox snorted, I wondered why I had thought this was such a good idea.

Sonny was good to his word. He held Old Sox steady and cooed softly to her as he led us around the corral.

"How're you feeling? Ready to take the reins?" he asked after what seemed like forever. I didn't want to say yes, but I wanted to please Uncle Sonny, and I hoped if I did, I wouldn't be so afraid near horses in the future.

My uncle stayed close by in the corral. I was sure Old Sox could smell my perspiration and hear me breathing hard. She started walking faster, either because she was bored or she sensed my fear. In a firm voice, Sonny assured me I was doing fine and reminded me he was right there with me. Old Sox began to trot even faster. A wave of fear washed over me around the time we came close to the fence and my right leg scraped up against it. Old Sox must have felt me loose in the saddle. She started to go faster. I don't know if I decided to get off while the horse was moving or if I lost my balance and fell off. Whatever the reason, I fell, still holding on to the reins.

Petrified and sure I was a goner, I heard Uncle Sonny yell, "Let go of the rope or you're going to get dragged through the shit! Let go. Let go of the rope!"

I followed his directions. Nothing was hurt but my pride.

———

Years later, when I turned fifty, I decided to take riding lessons. One afternoon while I was riding in the arena, the trainer told me to take the horse to a trot. A group of riders returning from the trails in the forest preserves filed into the bleachers to watch my lesson. As they got settled, my horse began to trot faster.

Just as I fell off my horse, someone yelled out, "Tyra, what's your secret to riding?"

I stood up, brushed myself off, and yelled back, "On is good. Off is bad!"

I was sure Uncle Sonny would have been proud of how I fell.

Throughout my life, I've heard Uncle Sonny's voice in my head whenever I've found myself overzealously determined to accomplish a goal or I've realized I was so sure of my approach that I had not clearly considered others' input or possible compromises. I woke up the morning after my dream about Uncle Sonny feeling sure that going to The Menninger Clinic was the right thing. Bingeing, purging, sleeping all day, and hating myself for not being able to care for my baby flooded my soul with disgust and disrespect for the person I had become.

Finally, it was time to go to Topeka. I had written Larry and told him the doctor recommended that I go to the Clinic. I assured him Laura would be in good care since she would stay with the Woodrows, her regular babysitters and longtime family friends. In typical Larry style, he was his supportive self. "Do what the doctors tell you, Tyra. Do good and get well so you can meet me in Hawaii for R&R. I believe in you," he assured me. If only he could come home, I would be fine, I told myself over and over. But I said nothing.

I worried throughout the entire flight, about leaving Laura, and about the possibility that Larry might be killed in Vietnam and that I would lose him like I'd lost Daddy from a heart attack. My thoughts served up every possible worst outcome I could imagine. What if I was beyond help, like some of the people in the state mental hospital in Big Spring not far from Seminole? What if I couldn't get better?

Mother and I took a cab from the airport in Topeka to the local Holiday Inn. Mother struck up a conversation with the cab driver that focused on the history of Topeka, the capitol of Kansas, and the local university, Washburn. The next morning, the Clinic staff sent a cab for us. The receptionist explained we were early and suggested we might like to walk around the campus. As we walked down the manicured sidewalks, I noticed most of the people were walking in groups or pairs. Mother was impressed with the greenhouse. Her flower beds at home were magnificent. She loved gardening and appreciated that everyone at Menninger seemed to be working, not lying in bed all day. I resented that she didn't understand why I stayed in bed.

Mrs. Johnson, an aide on the unit where I would live, appeared when we returned from our walk. I worried about what was next as we followed her to a small conference room. As we entered, a slender gray-haired man rose from an oblong table.

"Good morning." Dr. Roberts greeted us with a warm sure handshake. "Please sit down. I'm Dr. Roberts. I'll be your house doctor." When he asked me to tell him about myself, I diminished my persistent fear and dread. I didn't tell him how lost and uncertain I felt and how I lived in a gray hopeless world. I didn't mention my nose and how it burned all day long like an anxiety thermometer. I told him I was there because I wanted to get better. I wanted to meet Larry for R&R in Hawaii and I wanted to take care of our baby.

Without warning, he told me to say good-bye to Mother and asked Mrs. Johnson to take me to the ward. My legs grew numb as I told Mother good-bye, hugged her quickly so she wouldn't see me cry, and asked her to tell Laura I loved her. Mother looked as surprised as I felt. She hugged me back and told me she loved me as Mrs. Johnson opened the conference room door and ushered me down the hall.

Mrs. Johnson led me to the ward. She unlocked the door with the keys she carried on her wrist and said, "This will be home while you're here. Your room's down this hall."

I had asked to come to Menninger. I wanted to get better, but as the heavy door slammed behind me, my internal voice screamed, "What have you done, you idiot? You must be crazy!"

---

Years later, I look back on that slamming door and realize Menninger was my last hope. In that moment, I wanted to scream, "Just lock me up!" as it raced through my mind over and over. Over the years, I've remembered that October day many times. I am still overwhelmed with gratitude and always will be. Walking through that heavy door as it slammed behind me was the first real step toward my recovery.

# YOUR TURN

..........................................

We all have struggles throughout our lives regarding major decisions or choices we face. An internal voice or our heart nudges us from within, our intuitive guidance system giving us information anytime we need it. Write about a time in your life when your intuition had information for you. Use these guidelines to tell your story.

**What was it like at the beginning of the story?** Include the facts—where you were, when the event took place, who was there, and how you felt.

**What happened?** Write the story like you would tell it verbally. Use active language and give examples. Include as much detail as possible to vividly recreate the scene. Most important, what was the issue? Was there a problem, a tragedy, a celebration?

**What was it like at the end of the story?** For me, the most important stories are those that teach us something. What did you learn from your experience? In writing *Where the Water Meets the Sand*, I realized that many of the lessons I learned in childhood, I later utilized and appreciated as an adult.

# CHAPTER 4:

# Freedom from Addictions

·····························································

I know firsthand what a vise grip addictions and self-harming behaviors can have on a person because I struggled for years with alcohol dependency, bingeing and purging, and cutting. My troubled relationship with food, and my rituals to avoid pain and fear with it, began when I was nine, the year my father died and my mother went back to college. Daddy's death left an emptiness in my heart. I coped by sneaking food from the refrigerator and used my weekly allowance to purchase potato chips, ice cream, candy bars, and Coca-Cola on the way home from the library. I started experimenting with beer at the age of twelve and began drinking alcohol seriously at fifteen.

I made the hard decision to admit myself to The Menninger Clinic after Larry deployed to Vietnam. At the Clinic, I spent eight months in treatment for severe anxiety and clinical depression. Talk therapy, art therapy, and music lessons helped me begin to consciously acknowledge the events and stories surrounding my bingeing and purging addiction, as well as my addiction to cutting. I wrote out my true stories and sometimes read them to my therapist. I pounded and sculpted clay and played volleyball and the piano. There, I came to understand that my addictions were substitutes and decoys masking feelings of despair and grief about losing my father as a child, and my fear that my husband would be killed in the Vietnam War. My willingness to acknowledge the truth of my addictions and talk about them were the first steps to healing.

———

I'll never forget the day Dr. Roberts told me we wouldn't grab a cup of coffee and go for a walk on the beautifully manicured campus for my daily session with him. A voice in my head screamed, *Larry's dead*. Dr. Roberts told me Larry had been killed on February 19, 1971. Laura, our baby girl, would celebrate her second birthday on March 4, in just twelve days. My heart broke for her and for me. More than anything, I wanted Larry home with me and I wanted Laura to have her daddy. My worst fear had come true. Larry had been killed in battle. Representatives from the air force would bring the "regret letter" to me when I was ready. Years later, I realized how very fortunate I was to be at the Clinic with a tremendous support system when Larry was killed. For that I am forever grateful.

———

After I left residential treatment at Menninger and continued outpatient therapy, I replaced the activities I'd done in the hospital with structured home activities. Writing was one of them. I poured my grief out onto the page. I wrote stories about Laura and me so she would have them when she got older. I yelled at Larry on the page for getting himself killed and I begged him for forgiveness for being angry at him. I wrote about what our life could have been like if he had lived, and I told him how proud I was of his service to his country.

I shared my writing with my therapist and often read it out loud. He told me to keep writing.

## BINGEING AND PURGING

After Larry left for Vietnam in 1970, I used binge eating and purging to relieve my escalating anxiety, depression, and the sense that all the fear building up inside me would blow off the top of my head. I also learned that bingeing and purging increased the endorphins in my body, which brought on a sense of well-being. I ate to get full. *What else is there?* I'd ask myself. *I'm only twenty-three years old, and Larry's in Nam and may not come home. I've left my baby girl with friends because I can't get through a day without bingeing and purging and sometimes cutting*, I'd whine internally. This addiction grew out of emotional and tangible losses. Filling myself with fattening, sweet, and rich fried foods was a physically satisfying, nurturing antidote. I told myself I didn't care how I looked or how unhealthy my behavior was, but I hated myself for gorging and for putting my fingers down my throat to make myself vomit.

During one of our sessions, my psychiatrist, Dr. Roberts, told me that a cafeteria worker had reported seeing me walk out of the dining room with a piece of pie hidden under my shirt.

"You don't have to hide food," Dr. Roberts assured me. "You're welcome to take as much as you want." He paused, and then continued. "The maids who clean your room have reported that your bathroom is splattered with vomit. They have requested that we put a toilet bowl brush and cleaning supplies in your bathroom so you can clean it yourself. They'll be happy to clean your toilet area when you stop vomiting."

I was mortified and apologized. I was emotionally fragile, and pleasing the person who I believed held the key to my getting well was the major impetus for the Herculean effort I made to refrain from purging. If I binged, I made myself sit on my hands until the compulsion to vomit subsided. I refrained from bingeing and purging because I dreaded having to confess to Dr. Roberts that I had let him down. As I became healthier, I realized I had learned not to let myself down most of the time, though I did have occasional slips.

After I was discharged from inpatient care and left the Clinic, I began analysis with a new psychiatrist. Laura came to live with me in the mobile home Larry had purchased for us before he left for Vietnam. I enrolled in Washburn University to complete my bachelor's degree. However, I continued to binge and purge off and on. There was no particular trigger, though as I have reflected back on that specific addiction, I know that it, like my other addictions, filled a void, a feeling of emptiness and loneliness. Afterward, I fell asleep and avoided feeling lonely, overwhelmed, and sad that Larry was never coming home. These slips did not occur regularly, and over time I simply stopped as I became more comfortable in my own skin. Taking care of Laura, making a life for us, and finishing my bachelor's degree were my priorities.

In my case, resorting to bingeing and purging, cutting, and alcohol provided a similar comfort. They all gave me something to do when I felt lonely, sad, and overwhelmed. All three provided an escape. Each addiction resulted in a chemical high. Bingeing and purging and cutting produced physical endorphins. Drinking alcohol added an external chemical that produced a high on many levels, although I perceived it to be more acceptable than my other addictions.

During the decade after I left The Menninger Clinic, from time to time I wrote my former social worker, Nolan Brohaugh. I sent him short essays on my recovery and gave updates about how I was doing. He shared my stories with his supervisor, and I was invited to speak at a Menninger-sponsored workshop in Aspen, Colorado, for social workers earning CEUs. I was thrilled for the opportunity to give back.

After sharing my story about my recovery from bulimia, I opened the floor to questions. One of the participants began, "I work on a locked unit for patients with eating disorders. Among the staff, we've struggled with a decision—whether to lock the community toilets on our unit, requiring patients to ask for permission to use the bathroom or not to lock the stalls. We are concerned that needing to ask for permission hurts their self-esteem. What are your thoughts?"

I immediately saw myself kneeling on the floor, head hanging over the toilet. Before I thought about it, emphatic words flew out of my mouth. "You have to decide which is worse for someone's self-esteem: having to ask to have the toilet stall opened, or suffering the self-imposed degradation of kneeling in front of a toilet bowl as if it is a shrine, their head hanging over it with their fingers stuck down their throat, vomit and filth running down their arms, spraying all over the toilet bowl and walls, and then working to clean it up before anyone notices.

"Then comes the guilt. They know they've given in to their addiction one more time, feel disgust and failure, and are exhausted. Bingeing and purging is an addiction like alcohol. The motions are different, but you get a high for a short while and then are overwhelmed with disgrace and the agonizing fear of being out of control." I stood quietly, amazed at my words and shocked that I had been so direct with a group of professional social workers.

After my talk, several members of the audience thanked me for my candor. I don't know if that was the right answer, but my response was honest. When I was an active bulimic, I was obsessed with my favorite sugary foods and fried foods buried with gravy. Even as I planned ways to get them, I dreaded the horrible ending of the ritual. It was as if the ritual was a play and I dreaded the last act: bowing before a toilet bowl, forcing my finger down my throat as vomit ran down my arm until I was exhausted and using the bowl as a pillow, knowing the tile floor and bowl had to be scrubbed as well as me.

"I've learned healthy self-esteem comes from within," I told the social workers at the workshop. "When people suffer with an addiction like bulimia, they are unable to control their need to act on their compulsion to binge and purge. If they were able to refrain from bingeing and purging, they wouldn't need to have the toilet stalls locked. By leaving the toilet stalls open, it feels to me like you're setting them up for failure. Locked toilet stalls prevent patients from going through the humiliation of acting on their compulsions. In my opinion, locked toilet stalls telegraph that you care about them and have put safety measures in place to keep them safe from hurting themselves until they are healthy enough to refrain from acting on their addictive compulsion. The message to them is you believe in them and know they can and will overcome their bingeing and purging behavior. Locking the toilet stalls is part of the protocols and a safety net to keep them safe until they are able to overcome their bulimic addiction."

## CUTTING

Whenever I felt a compulsion to cut my wrists, it was because I felt that if I took action and cut, the fear and pain would go away, like accounts of bloodletting in the old days. While at Menninger, I became very close to my house doctor, Dr. Roberts. He almost always stopped by for a session on Saturdays even though most patients saw their house doctors on weekdays only. One particular Saturday he didn't come. Feeling distraught, agitated, and fidgety, I tried to sleep through the weekend. I felt abandoned and couldn't help but focus on my fear that my husband wouldn't come home. Unrelenting thoughts of Larry's plane crashing and burning surged through my brain like electrical currents. I had to do something to stop them.

That night I stole an empty Coke bottle from the patient lounge and took it into my room. I broke it and used a shard to cut my wrists. I remember the immediate relief as I watched the blood drip from my wrist into the toilet. I stared down into the bowl, hypnotized by the swirling pink clouds, and rested my head on the toilet seat, no longer feeling alone, panicked, or crazy. I felt at peace.

Eventually I walked down to the nurses' office and showed one of the nurses. She immediately called Dr. Roberts, who insisted that she take me to see the medical doctor for patients at the Clinic.

The doctor was kind and compassionate. He didn't ask too many questions. Walking back to the ward after he had bandaged me up, I noticed the stars twinkling in the sky. I remembered Larry telling me that whenever I missed him I should look up and know that he would be seeing the same moon and stars from the other side of the world and would be thinking about me. I couldn't help but think, *Larry would be so sad if he saw me right now. I can't believe how careless I was tonight. I have to be even more focused on getting better—for myself and for my husband and our daughter.*

Dr. Roberts was waiting in my room. He looked painfully tired, his face drawn as I sat down on the bed. "What happened?" he asked. "What's going on?"

I sobbed and blubbered about my fear of losing Larry, my homesickness, and my longing for my daughter, Laura, whom I hadn't seen in four months. I felt so guilty. Her father was in Vietnam and her mother was in a mental hospital. Dr. Roberts assured me I was where I belonged and that Laura's life would be better because I would be able to care for her. As far as we knew, Larry was fine. That was all we had.

When patients hurt themselves, they were placed on "watch." All the furniture would be moved out of my room and I would have to sleep on a mattress on the floor. I would eat my meals on trays in my room instead of being allowed to go to the dining room.

"Please, please, don't treat me crazy," I begged Dr. Roberts through my tears. "If you do, I'll get crazy. I know what I did *looks* crazy, but I wasn't trying to kill myself. I just had to stop the pain. I'm just barely holding on. If you do this, I'm afraid I'll fall apart again."

Dr. Roberts finally said he would see if an exception could be made since this setback wasn't typical of my recent progress. Just before he left, he said, "Mrs. Hull, I believe in you."

The next morning, I was in the lounge when George, a fellow patient, came in for coffee.

"What's this?" he said. "Who moved the sodas? What's with this sign?"

I looked up from where I was seated in front of a half-finished puzzle.

"Tyra, do you know . . . Hey, what's happened to your arm?" He pointed at it. "Why is it bandaged up to your elbow?"

"It's because of me, George. I cut my wrist with a Coke bottle last night. I'm really sorry about the sodas being moved. I didn't mean it." I teared up. Although I'd managed to salvage most of my privileges, I had caused the entire ward to lose a significant one. Now, to drink a soda, each patient had to go to the nurses' station and request it. This event taught me the power of group pressure to encourage correct behavior. I've never forgotten it.

## ALCOHOL

Although my occasional slips with bulimia and cutting subsided over time after I left The Menninger Clinic, alcohol remained a problem for me.

In January 1978, on the first night I attended graduate classes at the University of Kansas where I was to earn my master's degree in school administration, the school canceled the last class of the evening due to a blinding snowstorm. My colleague and friend had agreed to carpool with me to classes for the entire semester. I drove my car that night while Claudia rode in the passenger seat. The snow was blinding on the two-lane highway from Lawrence to Topeka. Approximately three miles outside of Lawrence, a young man in his twenties under the influence of alcohol crossed the center line and crashed into my car head on. He was killed and his passenger suffered a broken leg. Claudia's right elbow was broken and she lost some of her teeth. I was not as fortunate. My body was lodged between my bucket seat and the windshield. I suffered a concussion and lacerations to the left side of my head as well as to my forehead and left eye. I remained in a coma for twelve days.

I awoke in the ICU, escorted back to consciousness by a host of butterflies the colors of the rainbow and brilliant gold. All I remembered was Larry's visit at the crash site. He had insisted that I go back to take care of Laura. My right ankle was crushed, bones in my left foot were broken, and my left wrist was fractured.

After daily physical therapy for a number of weeks, I was discharged from the hospital in a wheelchair and provided with a home health aide. Filled with resentment and dependent on my aide, I worried incessantly. Devastated and haunted to have been involved in a car accident that had taken a young man's life, I realized it could have been me under the influence of alcohol that night. By the grace of God, it wasn't me, but it could have been. My antidote was to insist that the health aide bring me a beer at exactly noon every day. I started back to work on crutches and attended the last class of KU's semester. After that, I made sure I didn't drink and drive, but I drank too much at night after I got home from work. I didn't drink because I enjoyed it. I drank to numb the stress and demons I still carried within me from losing Larry and Daddy and my weakness for being addicted to alcohol.

Like many alcoholics, I carried a list of hurts, disappointments, and resentments around with me like beads of angry pearls. Deep inside, I knew I had a problem with alcohol.

I received a reckless driving ticket and was required to attend a safe-driving course. A classy recovering woman told her story: how she admitted she had a drinking problem and how she got sober. She talked about a recovery group she attended and how her life had changed for the better. During one of those sessions, I knew I was like her when she drank. I was an alcoholic too. She was articulate, not like the stereotype of alcoholics I held. I decided to go to a support group for recovering alcoholics on July 1, 1981.

The first thing I was advised to do was to ask someone with sobriety to be my mentor. I asked Old Ira, one of my favorite wise old codgers. He cautioned all of us in the group not to judge some of the younger addicts for their use of hard drugs. Because of Old Ira, I understood that if those drugs had been available to me, I might very well have used them. I learned an addiction is an addiction is an addiction. Mine happened to be alcohol, bingeing and purging, and cutting.

I also met a gruff, older woman named Gracie, whom I eventually asked to be my mentor as well. Gracie was the personification of tough love. She repeatedly admonished me when I resisted attending meetings, saying, "Read the Book. Repeat the Serenity Prayer out loud five times when you wake up in the morning and five times before you go to bed at night. I recommend seven meetings in seven days for newcomers."

She was the epitome of a sober person, holding me accountable by insisting that we ride together to the meetings. "Hearing the stories of other addicted people will make you grateful," she reminded me.

Going to meetings felt like going home. My grandmother Nennie had taught me the Serenity Prayer when I was just a teenager because she believed I worried too much. Attending meetings with my mentor and repeating the Serenity Prayer made me feel close to Nennie.

When Old Ira died, I flew to Kansas for his funeral. It was packed with recovering alcoholics with years of sobriety under their belts, along with others just beginning on their path to recovery. Old Ira gave his life to helping others after he got sober, and even more after he retired. All these years later, when things feel especially hard, I can hear Old Ira's voice in my head: "I hope we'll see your dragging ass around here again."

# YOUR TURN

..............................................

My favorite two best tips on how to give up an addiction are:

1. Take one day at a time. If that doesn't work for you, break it down. Take one hour or even thirty minutes at a time.
2. Say the Serenity Prayer five times out loud in the morning when you get up and five times aloud in the evening before you go to bed.

For this chapter's writing exercise, if you're someone who wants to overcome an addiction or fervently hopes someone dear to you will overcome an addiction, name the addiction you want to overcome and write out what it is like now at the beginning of this journey you are on. If you're someone who has overcome an addiction or knows a loved one who has, name the addiction you or your loved one has overcome and write out what it is like now.

**What was it like at the beginning of the story?** Include the facts—where you were, when the event took place, who was there, and how you felt.

**What happened?** Write the story like you would tell it verbally. Use active language and give examples. Include as much detail as possible to vividly recreate the scene. Most important, what was the issue? Was there a problem, a tragedy, a celebration?

**What was it like at the end of the story?** For me, the most important stories are those that teach us something. What did you learn from your experience? In writing *Where the Water Meets the Sand*, I realized that many of the lessons I learned in childhood, I later utilized and appreciated as an adult.

# CHAPTER 5:

# Grief

················

The Menninger Clinic became my home away from home in 1970, when I was hospitalized for clinical depression after Larry left for Vietnam. I constantly worried about him and missed our baby daughter, Laura, but I knew the Clinic was where I belonged. I felt safe and trusted Dr. Roberts, my house doctor. I treasured my conversations with him. He enrolled me in daily sewing, art, and gym classes, as well as weekly piano classes, and made it clear I was to attend those classes because they were a major part of my therapy.

Gradually, I got my compulsions of cutting and bingeing and purging under control and grew to love and care about my new family, my fellow patients. The fears and despair I felt when I became a patient were replaced by hope.

I had earned individual privileges, meaning I could walk on the grounds, go to dinner in the dining room, and attend my classes, without an escort. Meeting my friends with the same privileges in the canteen reminded me of meeting a high school friend for lunch at the student union at Texas Tech University.

All was well until February 21, 1971. I was waiting for Dr. Roberts to arrive for our standing 3:00 p.m. session. We usually walked down to the cafeteria for a cup of coffee. But when I opened my door, he said, "We're not going for coffee today. We'll talk here."

"What's wrong?" But I was sure I already knew. An inner voice inside my head screamed, *Larry is dead!* Otherwise we would already be out the door, heading for the cafeteria. I plopped down on the twin bed in my room.

Dr. Roberts closed the door and pulled up the desk chair. "Mrs. Hull, your husband has been killed." Tears filled his eyes as he added, "Authorities have notified us that his plane crashed."

Time stood still. Larry's beautiful grin flashed in my mind's eye. I silently begged him, *No, no, don't leave us. Don't go. Please don't.*

I fell back onto the bed, curled my knees to my chest, and wrapped my arms around them tight. If I didn't move, perhaps Dr. Roberts's horrific news was a nightmare. *If only I could wake up.*

Dr. Roberts sat silently as Daddy, both my grandfathers, my uncle, and now my beloved Larry trudged through my memory.

Still lying in the fetal position, I lamented, "Larry's dead, like my daddy is dead." Firmly yet kindly, Dr. Roberts confirmed the news. "Yes. Your husband has died in Vietnam. His plane crashed. Your father died of a heart attack when you were a child." Dr. Roberts spoke slowly.

I could still see my father lying in his casket in the funeral home. At his visitation, I moved a chair close to the casket and climbed up on it so I could kiss Daddy good-bye.

At least Dr. Roberts was saying the words, not like when Daddy died and no one would speak the truth.

"Your husband has been killed in Vietnam," Dr. Roberts said again. "I don't know any more of the details, but when you feel ready, officers from Forbes Air Force Base will deliver the official letter."

Before Dr. Roberts left to go on rounds, he emphasized that he had made arrangements with the nurses for me to use the private phone in the phone booth outside the nurses' station.

"I'll stop by again before I leave the ward to see how you're doing," he promised as he closed the door to my room quietly.

A brutal fight ensued between the part of me that wanted to stay curled up in a ball and sleep through the rest of my life, and the part that insisted I be brave and strong and stay in the present.

I was at Menninger. Larry was dead. Laura had just lost her daddy, just like I had as a child. But Laura wasn't even two years old. She wouldn't remember playing on the floor with him and the times he tickled her, while blowing wet kisses on her tummy.

My body went numb from head to toe while in my mind reality began to set in, accompanied by a powerful longing. I would have given anything to talk to my husband right then.

I walked down the hall to the pay phone. I couldn't speak with Larry, but I could call my mother. The least I could do was make Larry proud. He had given his all, and I had a job to do.

I called Mother, but she didn't answer. I called one of her best friends who owned a restaurant where the news of the day was the topic at most tables and booths. I asked Josephine to put out the word in our small town. "Please have Mother call me at Menninger, it's important," I whimpered, trying not to cry. I asked Josephine to write down the pay phone number and share it with anyone who might run into Mother in town.

Dr. Roberts was good to his word and stopped by my room before he left. An air force officer from Forbes Air Force Base outside of Topeka had asked to deliver the official letter to me.

"How do you feel about that?" Dr. Roberts asked. "You don't have to answer today," he assured me.

"I want it as soon as they can deliver it. I want to know what happened to Larry. When can they come? Tomorrow?"

"I recommend we make it day after tomorrow. That will give you time to gather yourself and to think of any questions you want to ask them."

The Menninger staff told the other patients about Larry's death. It seemed as if the entire ward reached out to me, no matter how intrusive some of their illnesses were or how severe and unusual their symptoms. All who were able met in the patient lounge and invited me to join them. One of my favorite patients, Penny, knocked on my door and invited me down to listen to a new album by James Taylor, *Fire and Rain*.

Good to his word, Dr. Roberts arranged with officers from Forbes Air Force Base to hand deliver the official letter informing me that Larry had been killed in action. The letter said that Larry's plane had been shot down on February 19, 1971, two days before I was informed of his death. Dr. Roberts explained that the Menninger staff had taken the extra time to verify Larry's death and not risk giving me devastating information that was not accurate.

The letter said that Larry was killed in Southeast Asia. Due to hostile enemy fire, it was impossible to retrieve my husband's remains. I was overwrought and already emotionally fragile before this heartbreaking news, yet I determined that I would represent Larry with grace and bravery.

I decided to call the colonel who'd written the regret letter.

When his secretary answered the phone, I said, "Ma'am, my name is Tyra Hull. I need to talk with the colonel, please."

"May I ask your business?" she asked. "May I help you?"

"The colonel sent me a letter that says my husband, Lieutenant James L. Hull, was shot down in Vietnam and his body wasn't retrieved due to enemy fire," I explained. "I don't know what to do. I'm in a mental hospital and I need to talk to the colonel. I have to ask him if I should wait to have a funeral until Larry's body comes back or if I should have a memorial service now. Please tell him I need to talk to him," I pleaded.

"I'll see if he's available," she responded.

Immediately, the colonel came on the phone and asked if he could help.

"Sir, my name is Tyra Hull and I live at The Menninger Clinic, a mental hospital, in Topeka, Kansas. My husband is First Lieutenant James L. Hull. Officers from Forbes Air Force Base delivered a regret letter saying that Larry's plane was shot down in Vietnam and his remains could not be retrieved due to heavy enemy fire. I don't know what to do. My family lives in Texas and Larry's parents live on the air force base in

Guam. I need to have a memorial service or a funeral for Larry. Should I wait until Larry's remains come home or should I have a memorial service?"

I took a deep breath and waited.

"Mrs. Hull, you need to have a memorial service for your husband. Make it as much like a funeral as you can," the colonel advised. "We don't know when Lieutenant Hull's remains can be recovered, or if they will ever be. Call me again if you have other questions. Air force personnel at Forbes Air Force Base in Topeka will help you make arrangements for flying to Texas, and officers at Reese Air Force Base in Lubbock will assist you once you arrive there. I am sorry for your loss, and assure you that air force personnel will be there to help you get through this very difficult time."

"Thank you for your assistance and for your service," I responded and hung up.

I was tormented that Larry's remains were not able to be returned. I had promised him he would be buried at Arlington but that was impossible. I flew home to Texas with a psychiatric aide as my escort. The one good thing was I got to see our baby girl. I agonized over whether Laura would remember me after being apart for five months, and I was elated when she threw her arms around me as soon as she saw me.

I organized a memorial service as much like a funeral as I could at the First Baptist Church where I grew up. I worked with the local florist to create a large flower arrangement at the front of the church in place of a casket. After the service, the caravan of cars attending Larry's service drove out to the cemetery where my father was buried for a twenty-one-gun salute. Larry's mother, father, and younger brother were front and center with my family. Even some of Larry's Alabama relatives attended. My extended family were all there as well.

Two days after the memorial service, the aide and I flew back to Kansas. Going back to Menninger felt like going home. I didn't have to look right or act right. I was encouraged to talk about my sadness. I was at the best possible place to be after losing my beloved husband.

It still worried me that Larry was not buried at Arlington like he had requested, but I'd done all I could do. In spite of the unlikely odds, I still believed that one day Larry would be buried at Arlington.

One night in 2006, a sergeant at Lackland Air Force Base called to tell me that Larry's remains were coming home after thirty-five years. Finally, I was going to have the chance to keep my promise and bury him at Arlington.

I couldn't sleep that night. Instead, I sat outside on my front porch and wrote the following poem. I didn't think about why I was writing it. It was something I had to do. I still read it from time to time and wonder, *What does this poem mean? Why does it matter? What is my connection to Larry now that he is gone? What is the loss of a loved one? Do we miss them literally or do we miss our fantasies of what we might have had? If we carry them in our hearts, are they really gone?*

## IN A BOX

*Larry, they called,*
*Said you were coming home in a box,*
*Six months to a year from now,*
*Whatever's left,*
*Last night,*
*I slept better than all of the nights over the last 35 years,*
*Something about them picking you up,*
*Putting you all in one place,*
*Whatever's left,*
*Not strewn over the jungle floor,*
*Not scattered,*
*Getting you all in one place,*
*Whatever's left,*
*Bringing you home,*
*Not left alone in the dark,*

*In the jungle,*
*Whatever's left,*
*Some of your bones are in a box in Hawaii,*
*Your Laotian bones are on their way,*
*To join those rescued thirteen years ago,*
*Waiting in Hawaii,*
*Whatever's left,*
*I feel anxiously peaceful,*
*Laura and I may get you back,*
*All in one place,*
*Whatever's left*
*I might get you back,*
*All in one place,*
*Whatever's left,*
*All your bones in one place,*
*In one box,*
*I wait for their return,*
*Whatever's left,*
*I can put all the broken pieces of my heart,*
*Labeled with your name,*
*In the box,*
*On the shelf,*
*In my mind,*
*In one place,*
*Where I can find them,*
*Whatever's left,*
*In one place,*
*Not strewn all over my world,*
*Past, present, future*
*Memories of you,*

*In a box on a shelf in my mind,*
*Where I can find them,*
*I'll take it down,*
*Remove the lid,*
*Touch and remember,*
*The box,*
*On the shelf,*
*In my mind,*
*I wait for the return of your bones,*
*In a box,*
*In one place,*
*All that is left.*

In 2006, Larry's funeral was held in the chapel at Arlington National Cemetery. He was buried with full military honors. Keeping my promise to Larry mattered more than I could even have imagined. I still have the list of goals and other promises we wrote out when we married. It's kept me going. To this day, I pull out that list and refer to it. And some days when I'm mulling over a problem, I still hear Larry's voice telling me, *Don't worry, Tyra, it'll all work out,* and I believe him.

Larry's death was one of the many losses I suffered throughout my life, beginning with my father's death and continuing with the deaths of a baby cousin, a teenage cousin, two grandfathers, and soon after, the loss of the baby I gave up for adoption, followed by the deaths of both of my grandmothers, five uncles, my brother, stepfather, and finally my mother, over a span of sixty-two years.

## LOSING MOTHER

It was 12:41 a.m. on a Thursday when I called my sister and said, "Mother just passed." Saying the words out loud didn't seem real. But it was true. Mother was gone. I sobbed like a baby. Mama, gone. How could that be?

After Leon, my stepfather, died in September of 2015, Mother said, "Why am I still here? All of my younger brothers are gone and I'm still here. I'm the oldest and I'm still here."

I grieved for her before she passed. I grieved for her loneliness, for her sadness, and I grieved for her dependence on caregivers and my sister and me.

Mother was a proud, independent woman. She loved to putter in the garden and grow okra, tomatoes, squash, and sunflowers as tall as me. Once she declined and was trapped in her frail, failing body, I was torn between, "God, don't let her die," and, "God, don't let her suffer."

On one visit to Seminole before Leon passed, Mother and Leon showed me two black garment bags in their bedroom closet. "We've packed the clothes we want to be buried in," Mother said. "Everything each of us will need is here." I peeked inside Mom's garment bag and saw pink. *Of course*, I thought as I zipped up the garment bag, *Mother always loved pink dresses and pink roses.*

We took Mother's garment bag with her to the care facility. When the funeral home came to transport her body after she died, they asked if we had her clothing. We did.

I was stunned as I stepped up to Mother's open casket at the funeral home in our hometown. For her last public appearance, she had chosen a pink dress with a fitted bodice and a lace cummerbund, accompanied by a matching neck scarf. Her long sleeves were pink chiffon with covered buttons at the wrist. Mother usually chose tailored suits and dresses with subtle trimming. I wondered when and how she had purchased the pink dress.

During the visitation, one of Leon's daughters-in-law said something like, "Now we know what the dress was for. She sent me a photo of this dress cut out of a store catalogue in Lubbock and asked me to purchase it and mail it to her."

For the most part, Mother and Leon had been housebound for months before Leon died and Mother had been in the care center in Boerne for over a year. But Mother was an independent, self-sufficient woman as long as she could be.

Hearing the story of how Mother managed to select and purchase the dress she wanted to wear for her last debut makes me smile. This example of her independence, her tenacity, and her warmth continues to give me comfort. She took care of business until she couldn't, and then turned it over to God.

Tears still well up in my eyes when I least expect it, and my heart is desperately sad. I frequently sob out loud when I am alone. I miss her and remember the difficult times: Daddy's death, her drive alone to the hospital to have my baby sister after he died, the trip to escort me to The Menninger Clinic and my brother's death.

When I am overcome with sadness, the thought of Mom's pink dress makes me smile and leads me down a different road, one of pride in my mother's strengths. She was independent and still taking charge until she couldn't anymore. She died with grace and dignity at age ninety-four.

She used to tell me, "The least we can do is look right and act right." Mother did, until the end.

---

I have struggled to be at peace with the loss of those I love and to find a peaceful coexistence with death's ultimate reality. Each of the losses I have suffered has taught me not to take loved ones for granted. I have faith that this life is not the end of our journey, and I have found tremendous comfort in that, as well as in learning some of the following steps that have helped me turn my grief into strength:

## 7 HEALING STEPS

### 1. Say the Serenity Prayer.
I say this five times out loud in the morning and at night. It is my mantra and helps me remember to take one day at a time.

### 2. Do things to lighten your day.
I listen to music, play with my dog, go for walks, read, and look at favorite photos.

### 3. Write.

I write out my feelings, write what I am grateful for, write down the good times I remember, and I write to address the guilt that creeps up through grief.

### 4. Admit that you may feel relief.

I counsel myself that although Mother is gone, she is no longer suffering.

### 5. Breathe deeply.

I sit with my grief, breathe deeply and let the tears wash out the hurt.

### 6. Drink a cup of coffee.

I have an imaginary talk over a cup of coffee with the person who has passed. In the case of Mother, she would say, "Get busy, don't waste the precious time you have."

### 7. Sometimes just lie in bed.

I give myself permission to be still. I wait until I am bored and then I get up and do one or more of the above.

# YOUR TURN

As individuals, we all grieve differently. There is no right or wrong way to grieve. Each of us reacts uniquely to the loss of someone we love—a partner, a friend, a pet, or even a job. Grief is an emotional reaction to loss, but many of us experience a physical change in our bodies too. I often feel that for me, because of losing so many loved ones in my life, especially as a child and young person, I have developed an unintentional path or ritual in my brain that takes over when I lose someone or something that I treasure. I have included these rituals above. I am certain that delayed grief over the loss of my father when I was nine contributed to my despair and fear that I would lose Larry when he deployed to Vietnam. I lived in fear that he would be killed in the war. When I received the news that his plane had been shot down and that he was dead, the fear and anxiety that I would lose him subsided, and though I was filled with sadness and grief, I moved on by getting busy. I modeled my life's work on accomplishing the goals we had promised one another we would accomplish. Larry's death was horrible. Yet the reality of his death relieved me of the fear that I would lose him. The nightmare was over.

Use the following guidelines to tell your own story or stories about grief:

**What was it like at the beginning of the story?** Include the facts—where you were, when the event took place, who was there, and how you felt.

**What happened?** Write the story like you would tell it verbally. Use active language and give examples. Include as much detail as possible to vividly recreate the scene. Most important, what was the issue? Was there a problem, a tragedy, a celebration?

**What was it like at the end of the story?** For me, the most important stories are those that teach us something. What did you learn from your experience? In writing *Where the Water Meets the Sand*, I realized that many of the lessons I learned in childhood, I later utilized and appreciated as an adult.

CHAPTER 6:

# Moving On

..............................

Even though Larry's death was devastating, I felt such gratitude toward him for buying the trailer house for Laura and me to live in if he didn't return from Vietnam. When it was time for me to be discharged from The Menninger Clinic, Dr. Roberts gave his approval for the air force sergeant from the local Forbes Air Force Base in Topeka to meet with me and assist me in making arrangements for the trailer to be moved from Texas to Topeka.

I also decided to enroll at the local university, Washburn, to continue my degree in education. Each time I made a decision—regarding where Laura and I would live, to enroll in school, about a date to move out of the hospital—I felt more and more capable and sure of myself. Once all of these matters were in place, I was discharged. I had lived at the Clinic for a total of eight months.

I asked to go to the rose garden for my last session with Dr. Roberts. We discussed the disdain I'd held for the rose garden when I was first admitted to the hospital. The first time Dr. Roberts took me there, I told him, "Roses remind me of death. Growing up, we had perfect roses only when someone died. When Daddy died, we had perfect roses. When my grandfathers and uncles died, we had more roses. There were roses when my baby cousin drowned. When my younger cousin ran her car into a tree and died, we had more roses. I hate roses. Their sweet smell makes me sick."

"What's changed?" Dr. Roberts asked me now.

"My perspective has changed," I explained. "Roses symbolized death when I came to Menninger. They reminded me of my fear of losing Larry, and of all the people in my family who had died. The roses haven't changed, but what they symbolize has. My work in therapy has taught me to look for new perspectives and new possibilities."

We sat quietly for a while. When I first arrived at Menninger, I'd felt uncomfortable sitting in silence with someone. That last day, sitting quietly with Dr. Roberts felt like a prayer. I had felt loved and accepted at the Clinic. I had also learned I could change my perspective; I could make a conscious decision to look for and focus on the good in my life.

"Roses once represented death for me. Today, they represent hope."

After I left the Clinic, I completed my bachelor's degree at Washburn University and was hired as a middle school teacher in Topeka Public Schools, then got my doctorate at Kansas University and took a job in Highland Park, Illinois, as director of instruction in the school district. Leaving friends in Topeka and moving with my teenage daughter to a Chicago suburb was frightening and lonely. Laura was a high school sophomore, a difficult age to change schools and move to a community where she knew no one. However, I was ambitious and anxious to build my résumé and to pursue my dream of being a superintendent of schools. That kept me going.

Six years later, I moved to Stoughton, Wisconsin, to accept my first position as superintendent of schools. Although initially I worried that I couldn't meet the requirements of the job, over time, I grew comfortable and began to thrive in my role. The community, teachers, and board members were fantastic, but I was still lonely. I missed Chicago and my friends, and by then Laura had enrolled in college on the

East Coast. There were days when I felt as if I were totally alone in the world, simply because nothing except the school business was familiar.

Each time I moved, my sense of loss returned. Yet I continued to move on, following my dreams. Two years later, I moved back to Illinois to be superintendent of schools in River Forest. I remained there for twelve years, until I retired. Each time I moved forward with a more lucrative job promotion, the knowledge that Larry was with me and that I was never alone gave me the courage I needed to keep going.

In 1993, Laura and I flew to Washington, DC, to see Larry's name on the Vietnam Wall and to meet up with two of the men who'd flown with him. Colonel Tom Yarborough's and Archer Battista's accounts of their relationships with Larry confirmed that Larry had friends while overseas who'd cared about him, that he loved to fly, and that he was brave. Both men took great care to make sure Laura knew how proud he was of her. Making contact and sharing stories about Larry was amazing and healing for Laura and for me.

## MOVING ON FROM ALCOHOL ADDICTION

I took my first sip of beer as a teenager. It tasted terrible. I held my nose while I drank it and immediately pushed a mouthful of potato chips down my throat to dull the aftertaste. There was a cadence to the ritual: one long draw of beer from the can, followed by one huge mouthful of potato chips; one slug of beer, another mouthful of potato chips, time after time.

I soon got used to the taste as I began to focus on the ritual, and before long, beer was my new best friend. My grades began to drop, especially my sophomore year. I didn't care. I didn't spend as much time hanging out with my friends. I didn't care. By the end of my junior year, I had failed most of my classes and was on a collision course. I missed Daddy, I was mad at the world, and I loved the way beer made me feel. Although it never tasted good, I drank more and more of it.

Driver's education was required my freshman year, and I earned my driver's license at the age of fourteen. The more belligerent I became, the more I wanted to be alone. The more I wanted to be alone, the more I drank. I begged Mother to loan me the family car to go to the school library in the evenings to study, and instead I headed for the New Mexico state line for beer. I wondered if Mother really believed I was going to the library, but she must have hoped I was. Brazen and unafraid, I pulled up to the drive-in liquor store and ordered a six-pack. If I had taken a "'sick day" from school, after returning to my hometown, I'd frequently drive out to Daddy's grave. Mother, my brother, and I had chosen a bench with Daddy's name, *Decker*, on the seat. I was nine when Daddy died. By the time I was a teenager, the mimosa tree we'd planted, one of Daddy's favorite trees, barely shaded Daddy's bench. I sat on it, drank my beer, and told him my troubles: how much I missed him and how different I was sure my life would have been if he hadn't died.

Skipping school and visiting Daddy with a beer in my hand made me feel less lonely. It became a habit, one I looked forward to. In my day-to-day life, I missed Daddy more than ever, but at his grave, where his headstone said, *To Live in Hearts We Leave Behind Is Not to Die*, I felt safe.

———

I barely graduated from Seminole High School in 1965 and enrolled as a freshman at Texas Tech in Lubbock, Texas. Soon afterward I met Larry Hull, a boy more thoughtful and gracious than any I had ever known.

Larry invited me to a Sigma Chi party. As soon as we arrived at the party, Larry whispered, "Be careful of the punch. The gossip is someone may spike it with Everclear."

Not wanting to sound naïve, I didn't ask, *What is Everclear?*

Larry and I stayed together during most of the party, except for one time when some of the guys ended up visiting while their dates, a group of young women and I, sat on a couch talking. I knew none of them but joined in the conversation, though it felt frivolous to me. They were drinking punch and insisted that I trade the whiskey sour that Larry had mixed for me for one glass of punch. Wanting to fit in and assuming one glass of anything couldn't hurt, I said yes.

The punch was strong but tasty. As we visited, I sipped slowly. The girls and I split up, and Larry joined me. We agreed we'd had enough and headed over to some friends' house. Not long after arriving, I started to feel queasy. I asked Larry to take me home. As soon as he opened my car door and started around to his driver's side, I threw up on my turquoise satin dress with pearl trimming.

"Oh my God," I said. "What do we do now?" My lips started to tremble, and I thought, *This is disgusting. I can't believe I just ruined my dress and vomited in front of Larry, someone I'm falling in love with.*

"No worries. We'll drive to the service station. We'll get you all cleaned up," Larry, calm and cool, said. "I knew that punch was bad news."

Larry helped me wash up, though I trembled, shook, and stuttered as if I had come undone. He was so deft and tender. From that evening on, Larry mixed my drinks and brought me my beer. Larry didn't drink much, and when I was with Larry, I didn't either. I didn't need to.

After his death, though, I began to drink more and more. Not quite three years after Larry was killed in Vietnam, I married a man named Kenneth. I missed Larry and felt guilty about marrying again, but Kenneth was a good and kind man, who hit it off immediately with Laura, and I didn't want her to grow up without a father. I felt as if I didn't have the coping skills to raise her alone.

The longer Kenneth and I were married, however, the more I drank. I felt guilty about how much I still missed Larry, and my salve for that guilt was beer. For a while it seemed to soothe my soul, until it didn't.

A tragic event in January 1978 forced me to face my addiction to alcohol. I was the middle school coordinator for Topeka Public Schools. I loved the job and did it well. A colleague and I carpooled between Topeka and Lawrence, where we attended the University of Kansas. We took turns driving, and that night was my turn. After the first session of classes, the university canceled the last round of classes that night due to worsening weather predictions. My black Skylark Buick veered and slid toward the edge of the highway, especially on the icy curves.

Three miles outside of Lawrence, a young man's car crossed the center line and crashed into my car. The driver was killed and his passenger suffered a broken leg. I was pulled out of the wrecked car with the help of the Jaws of Life.

I do not remember the accident except for hearing Larry's voice: "You have to go back, you have to take care of Laura."

After twelve days in a coma, I finally opened my eyes in the hospital in Lawrence. My right ankle was crushed, bones in my left foot were broken, and my left wrist was broken. Most serious was the fracture of my forehead above my left eye. Almost half of my left eyelid was severed. When I finally woke up, I learned the young driver of the other vehicle had been drunk and was killed.

The first persons to visit me after I left the ICU unit and moved to a regular hospital room were my State Farm Insurance representative and my attorney. They asked me to tell them what happened.

"I can't tell you what happened, but I can show you what the car accident looked like from above if you'll give me a piece of paper and something to write with," I told them.

I drew two rectangular symbols representing my car and the one that had crashed into it as it had looked from my perspective, hovering above the accident scene. Both cars looked as if they'd been pushed to the edge of the highway of my traffic lane. Neither my attorney or my lawyer commented on my sketch, though both men asked if I remembered what happened. I shook my head.

My nights after the accident were restless and difficult. When I did sleep, nightmares about the crash and hearing Larry's voice at the site played in my head. My days were filled with the strenuous work of learning to pull myself out of my wheelchair and learning to walk during physical therapy twice a day. Once I learned to walk, I could go home. After six weeks, I was discharged from the hospital.

I left the hospital with a cast on my left arm, and casts on both legs. A home healthcare aide stayed with me during the days while I recuperated and learned to walk with crutches while still wearing three casts. During therapy, I struggled with the reality that I had been involved in a car accident that had killed another human being. I couldn't let go of the reality that a young man had died. Even though I wasn't drinking and driving, I knew I could have been. *It could have been you, drinking and driving*, my mind chastised me unmercifully. At noon, I allowed myself one beer. For me, drinking that one beer began with an honest belief that I could drink just one and prove to myself I was in control. Perhaps it was also a crutch, helping me get through the day—just like the crutches I now depended on to get to the bathroom or to the refrigerator for a drink. I lived in a state of terror and guilt, asking myself over and over. *What if I had been drinking and driving the night of the accident, instead of the other driver?* I could have been the one who'd crossed the center line of the highway. Beer was an antidote for my guilt about the situation. If I had taken a different route home from the university that night, I would not have been on that road when the young driver crossed the center line. He might have lived.

Over time, my one beer turned into two, and ultimately three. Alcohol numbed my disgust for the human being I had become. In my heart, I knew I was addicted to alcohol, but I didn't know what to do about it.

I finally returned to work wearing only one cast but still on crutches. I continued to drink at home, usually in the game room in our basement. On my TEAC reel-to-reel cassette player, I listened to the twenty-one double-sided tapes that Larry had recorded when he and his friends shared each other's record albums while in Vietnam. The air force had returned them to me after Larry was killed.

Two years later, in May 1980, I asked Kenneth for a divorce. Laura was devastated, but Kenneth didn't object. I think he knew that our relationship hadn't turned out to be what we'd hoped it would be. On some level, he may have sensed how much I still missed Larry. I have always been grateful that Kenneth still loved Laura and remained a main figure in her life for several years.

In 1981, one year after our divorce, I confronted my alcoholism. The husband of one of my school district colleagues was a recovering alcoholic, and I knew they attended a support group for alcoholics and their family members. I asked her if she could introduce me to a recovering alcoholic. A friend of her husband's invited me to lunch, brought me the AA Big Book for recovering alcoholics, and invited me to a meeting. I made a  decision to quit drinking on July 1, 1981.

When I attended support groups to overcome my addiction to alcohol, it was as if I had to give up my best friend. I thought that without alcohol I wasn't brave enough to live my life, raise Laura, and follow my career dreams. I learned that I depended on people, places, and things, and when I lost one or more of them, I struggled with the momentous loss and emptiness of moving through my life without those crutches.

On July 1, 2019, I will celebrate thirty-eight years of sobriety. I moved on from alcohol addiction, raised Laura, and accomplished my career dreams through hard work and wonderful opportunities served up by the universe. By invoking the Serenity Prayer five times aloud every morning and every night, I am reminded that I am not alone.

# YOUR TURN

........................................

Share a personal story or stories you have experienced that highlight a time in your life or the lives of your family when you had to "move on." Moving on can mean moving on and away from personal circumstances toward the realization of your dreams. Moving on may be a time you had to sacrifice by moving away from people you love for the opportunity to accept a new position, or moving to a part of the world where you've always wanted to live.

Moving on most often requires courage and trading in the familiar for a new opportunity. In my experience, change was always required of me when moving on, whether it was learning a new job, or leaving a comfortable job for an opportunity in a faraway place where I knew no one. Moving on meant sacrifice for the chance to make a dream come true. Moving on may mean you realize the road you have chosen no longer is satisfying. Your goals have changed and you want to choose a different path.

**What was it like at the beginning of the story?** Include the facts—where you were, when the event took place, who was there, and how you felt.

**What happened?** Write the story like you would tell it verbally. Use active language and give examples. Include as much detail as possible to vividly recreate the scene. Most important, what was the issue? Was there a problem, a tragedy, a celebration?

**What was it like at the end of the story?** For me, the most important stories are those that teach us something. What did you learn from your experience? In writing *Where the Water Meets the Sand*, I realized that many of the lessons I learned in childhood, I later utilized and appreciated as an adult.

## CHAPTER 7:

# Choosing Gratitude

.................................................

Gratitude is a choice. It's a choice that makes a difference. When I got sober in 1981, my mentor in the recovery support group taught me to make a gratitude list. Over the years, I've developed a pattern of writing down the things I have to be grateful for. I am often amazed at how long the list has become.

Gratitude is a powerful emotion that affirms the positive aspects of our lives as well as the people, community, and world around us. However, consciously instilling a habit of being grateful for life's circumstances can be hard at first. Like any habit, it takes practice. One way to start is by following the sage advice I received in the first alcohol support group I attended: "Fake it till you make it." Back then, I wasn't feeling particularly grateful to the universe for what it had handed me. However, over time I began to learn that, by choosing to focus on the positive aspects of my life, I felt better about my circumstances even though they hadn't changed in any substantive way. I also learned that expressing gratitude in thought, word, and deed began drawing people to me. Like the adage goes, "Honey catches more flies than vinegar."

The opposite of embracing gratitude is something called *stinking thinking*, another phrase I learned when I first got sober. *Stinking thinking* manifests when your brain ruminates on the worst possible outcomes of any situation or problem. It generates a barrage of negative self-talk, such as, "Everything in my life is all wrong, nothing I try to accomplish gets done, no one understands me, everything is hard, whine, whine, whine."

The problem with *stinking thinking* is that it triggers a continuous negative feedback loop that can incapacitate you. One bad thought triggers a memory of having been let down by someone you love, which dredges up a lifetime's worth of sediment about the wrongs you've experienced or perpetrated.

Years ago, I banished that negativity through daily recitation of the Serenity Prayer, a focus on helping others, and by filling my life with as many positive people as I can find. Keeping a list of friends, gifts and things I appreciate, and being around people who are part of my mutual support group, has created a shield around me. Volunteering has shifted my focus away from self and onto helping others.

Each of us has the power to rewire our brain, to fire its circuits for gratitude or negativity. It's a choice. When I choose being with others and reaching out to volunteer, I experience a sense of accomplishment and purpose. Going to the gym for rigorous exercise exhausts me physically, while leaving me grateful for my body's ability to exert itself.

Listening to music lifts my spirits and helps me acknowledge life's blessings and dwell on the goodness in my life. Even when I feel sad about those I've lost or who have passed from my life's horizon, I find that even my tears are in appreciation for having had the opportunity of knowing them and being enriched by them. Music has had this effect on me since I was a child and my father brought home a player piano he accepted as a trade-in for a car he sold. When I began taking piano lessons at the age of nine, I practiced the songs my piano teacher assigned since Daddy insisted on hearing me practice. After practicing my teacher's assignments, I played church songs from the Baptist hymnal, whose words had always made me feel as if they were personally meant for me when I heard them in church. I sang loudly as I played. It was as if I could go to church anytime I chose when I played and sang my favorite songs.

Even though I loved the piano and the way it made me feel when I mastered a difficult piece, I gave it up at the end of my junior year. That was the year my grades fell like a heavy bag of sand thrown out a third-story window. I was losing my way, drinking beer, and barely passing my classes. That was the summer I learned I was to become an unwed mother. During those difficult times, the songs I played on the car radio or my records made me feel less alone.

Music continues to be a mainstay in my life. On bad days, hearing a favorite song fills me with gratitude even if it's a sad piece. I often choose music that fits my mood. If I'm sad, I listen to sad music that reminds me that I am not alone. After I get over sitting on the pity pot, I play uplifting music that lifts my spirits. Melancholic music takes my soul to church and reminds me that everyone hurts. Uplifting music gives me hope. Both are important in my repertoire. My favorite songs have helped me through bad times and good times, and for that I will be eternally grateful.

## GRATITUDE IN PERU

Simon and Garfunkel's song "El Condor Pasa" has been a favorite of mine since I first heard it in 1971. The words remind me of Larry and of flying—literally, figuratively, and spiritually. The lyrics also reflect my gratitude—gratitude for the care I received at The Menninger Clinic, and for the freedom I earned after being discharged. "El Condor Pasa" became my personal hymn for the way it mystically tied together my freedom, Larry's love of flying, and the music he recorded in Vietnam that was shipped home to me after his death. Whenever I hear the lyrics, in my mind's eye I see Larry, his plane soaring above the mountains.

I see him piloting his small aircraft, dipping low and slow above the Laotian jungle during the Vietnam War before his plane was shot down. Of all the music that came back on the reel to reel tapes he recorded in 'Nam after he was killed, this song has helped me to understand his passion for flying and his decision to be a pilot.

In 2015 I decided to travel to Peru, which had been on my bucket list for years. I wanted to climb to the top of Machu Picchu. Peru's mountains are home to the famous Andean condor. When I saw real condors soaring and dipping and flying above the clouds so gracefully, and learned from native Peruvians that the path of the condor represents the intuitive, heartfelt, feminine aspect of life, I felt even closer to Larry. This personal odyssey made me feel as if I were receiving a magical infusion of hope and gratitude.

## GRATITUDE FOR CAREGIVERS

In 2007 I was diagnosed with chronic lymphocytic leukemia, which is manageable but not curable. Surgeons and nurses at Northwestern Hospital in Chicago performed a successful surgery and I began chemotherapy. After I moved to Texas, through connections with good friends, I began seeing Dr. Michael Keating at MD Anderson in Houston. He made my day during my first appointment when he said, "If you have to have cancer, you've got the best kind." When Dr. Keating gave me a big bear hug, I felt like everything was going to be all right.

As of 2018, it has been eleven years since my diagnosis. I now have a regular checkup every four to six months depending on the results of my most recent lab tests. I am no longer fearful but am overwhelmed with gratitude for all the fantastic caregivers I have. When I look back, the multitude of times I have been blessed are too many to count. I am so fortunate to have had the assets and connections to receive treatment at The Menninger Clinic as well as at MD Anderson. Mental illness and cancer don't play favorites, but there is help and a way forward, though it may not be what we envisioned.

When I was a young bride, Larry used to say, "Tyra, don't worry. It will pass. That doesn't mean XYZ will happen. It means just let whatever you're worried about pass right on through. Don't fight it. It will all work out."

And it has.

## GRATITUDE AT THE ROTARY HOUSE

Since 2010, I have stayed at the Rotary House Hotel, a lovely full-service hotel, dedicated exclusively to accommodate the needs of MD Anderson patients and their families. I am filled with gratitude that I have fantastic doctors and a place to stay that is familiar to patients at Anderson. Though it may seem unusual, I experience a sense of coming home there. The Rotary House's goal is to make patients and their families feel comfortable, as if we're at a home away from home, and they succeed in that. I can attest to the great service and accommodations made by the staff to make sure everyone feels welcome. When I arrive, most of the valets call me by my name. Several of the wait staff in the dining room know me. It's not unusual for one of them to bring me a menu and say, "Coffee, black?"

The Rotary staff regularly schedules a pianist to play patients' requested songs in the large atrium lobby. Singalongs erupt and often result in an introduction to a new friend. The conversation often turns to the question, "Why are you here?" It fills me with gratitude to feel safe enough to discuss my illness in detail, to realize that I am part of a community and not alone.

## GRATITUDE IN THE WAITING ROOM

In December 2016, young staffers strolled into the patients' waiting room at MD Anderson in Houston, schlepping cardboard boxes brimming with Christmas tree decorations. While we waited for our names to be called, other patients and I watched as they emptied their boxes and began trimming the tree in the corner of the room. A few of us in the waiting room began discussing the tree-trimming project as we interjected critiques of their work among ourselves. We began hanging handmade cancer awareness ribbons made of multicolored construction paper representing all cancers. The paper ribbons, a bit like icing on a birthday cake, heralded that this tree was special; it was a tree of hope and love. A few minutes later, the receptionist called my name and I went in for my appointment.

From the beginning, I have been astounded by the amazing work of the doctors, nurses, and staffers at MD Anderson. But I've drawn my personal strength from the example of hope from the community of patients I've met in the waiting rooms. The experienced know how it feels to get that dreaded diagnosis and move on with it. They make the newbies feel less vulnerable and less alone. In the waiting rooms we are all generous sharing our experiences, strength, and hope, even though some of us are struggling with difficult and unbelievable odds. Other patients told me right from the beginning what worked for them and the things they did to build hope and faith. Their courage, combined with great treatment from caregivers, especially amazing doctors, and support from family members and friends, demands that we choose to believe in the best possible outcome.

Choosing gratitude over fear is a decision we all make. It's a lesson I learned at The Menninger Clinic from my doctor and patient friends, and at MD Anderson. Fellow patients at both hospitals have taught me to do what the doctors tell me, to be grateful, and to recognize that choosing hope leads to confidence—confidence the doctors know what they're doing and confidence I have the best possible care.

Elated that after almost three hours all my appointments had gone well, I thanked God my CLL (chronic lymphocytic leukemia) hadn't required a full-body CT scan for several years. I stepped back into the waiting room, which was filled with a new crowd. The tree was finished and the decorators were nowhere in sight. The construction paper ribbons were all in place and looked great.

I wondered what the eightyish year-old woman accompanied by her daughter and son-in-law sitting just a few feet across from me would decide to tell her friends about her new cancer diagnosis.

"Mom," her daughter said, "the doctor said it was manageable, and he said it was treatable. Tell them it's treatable. That's all you have to say."

Her mother's response was one I had said myself when I was first diagnosed with cancer. "I just don't want them to think I'm dying. I can't take that."

Through the open door, I could see the back of a young woman pushing her mother's wheelchair onto the elevator. *I hope that went well*, I thought. I couldn't see their faces, but from our previous conversation, I knew the daughter was worried.

I stepped a few feet away from the tree and aimed my cell phone, careful to maintain the privacy of those standing in line at the registration desk. I snapped one more photo of the festive tree as new patients and their escorts watched.

A man named Mike jumped up from his seat, introduced himself, and added, "Here, let me take you by the tree. Okay?"

"Sure, I'd like that." I smiled back and handed him my phone. "I watched it being decorated but was called before they finished."

As I walked away, I knew it wasn't just the tree that I loved, but the community that it represented—the patient-driven, caring community. I loved that tree for what it stood for: hope, love, and courage.

In November 2017, Dr. Keating ordered another dose of chemo infusion for me. I had been fortunate and not required chemo for several years. I requested that the chemo be administered in San Antonio at an oncology clinic to avoid having to stay in Houston for several days. Dr. Keating agreed and coordinated my treatment with an oncologist in San Antonio. Lying back in the large lounge chair hooked up to the chemo drip, I slept sporadically, checked my Facebook page, and took my computer out so I could work on my weekly blog. Stuck in the same chair and unable to move around, I found myself remembering.

## GRATEFUL TO SERVE

I remembered childhood stories and wonderful memories of my time with my late husband, Larry. My mind took a tour of major events and smaller incidences that stuck in my head because of what I had learned over the years. Over the hours I sat there, I remembered things I hadn't thought of in years. Impacted by the holiday season, my mind wandered deep into my memory bank, bringing one particular Saturday evening to the forefront. My daughter, Laura, and I both attended the same church in Chicago. The church participated in a program with other churches, providing meals to homeless people in downtown Chicago on Saturday nights.

On the day I remembered so strongly, Laura went to the church early to work with the team responsible for making a huge kettle of soup. I joined the meal preparation team later that afternoon to make sandwiches and bag each meal.

We set up our station on the sidewalk in the heart of the city. The night was cold and rainy and, as I recall, we offered our special customers plastic rain capes.

I was positioned at the head of the serving line. As each customer approached the line, I welcomed them and went through the sandwich menu and fresh fruit choices. Next, they moved on to the soup kettle where Laura was serving.

"Good evening, sir," I greeted a man in the same way I had welcomed all of those who had preceded him. "We have bologna, chicken, and peanut butter sandwiches. We also have a variety of fruit for you to choose from. What would you prefer?"

The gentleman simply stood there gawking at me. I thought perhaps he hadn't heard me.

"Sir," I said again, "we have bologna, chicken, and peanut butter sandwiches. What will you have?"

After a long drawn out silence, the gentleman said, "Ma'am, I haven't been called 'Sir' in so long that I can't remember the last time." Tears welled up in his eyes.

I was so stunned by his emotional response that I stepped out from behind the serving table and put out my hand to shake his.

"My name is Tyra. What's yours?" I asked.

"I'm Matt," he said. Our hands clasped each other's.

"It's so nice to meet you, Matt. There's mustard or mayonnaise and hot coffee at the end of the line. Enjoy. And Matt . . . it's so good to talk to you."

Matt and the others who were served that night may have felt that they received gifts from us, but I left knowing that Matt and his friends were the givers. The gift was mine; I will never forget Matt.

Soon after I recalled Matt and his colleagues, the head nurse came to unhook the IV from my arm and I was discharged for the day. I was still grateful for Matt and that experience. It's always true that when I reach out to help others, it turns out they are the givers.

# YOUR TURN

UCLA's Mindfulness Awareness Research Center has verified that expressing grat-itude on a regular basis literally rewires our brains to make us feel happier. They verified that being happy gives us a sense of peace and tranquility and helps us avoid reacting negatively to difficult people or situations.

When I attended a support group to stop drinking alcohol, I realized that I often drank when I was sad, unhappy, and despondent, and I drank when I reached a goal and celebrated a milestone. I drank when I was happy and I drank when I was sad. I learned that I drank for three reasons: issues regarding people, places, and things. Yet over time, I realized people, places, and things in my life were the same things I loved, valued, and was grateful for.

During my quest for sobriety I began a daily ritual which I continue to this day, thirty-eight years after I got sober.

1. I say the Serenity Prayer five times aloud in the morning and in the evening.

2. I write down three things I am grateful for every day. I keep this daily log in a notebook or journal. I refer back to it when I want to feel grateful and when I feel negative and need a shot of gratitude. It seems most important to journal at the same time during the day so it becomes as routine as brushing my teeth.

3. I remember to tell the people closest to me that I appreciate them. I do it every day.

4. While I dress in the morning, I remind myself about something I have done for someone else recently or something of which I am proud.

Share a personal story or stories you have experienced that highlight a time in your life when you felt an overwhelming sense of gratitude. Did you have a physical reaction, such as goose bumps down your spine, or a flood of tears of relief when a difficult situation had passed and was over?

**What was it like at the beginning of the story?** Include the facts—where you were, when the event took place, who was there, and how you felt.

**What happened?** Write the story like you would tell it verbally. Use active language and give examples. Include as much detail as possible to vividly recreate the scene. Most important, what was the issue? Was there a problem, a tragedy, a celebration?

**What was it like at the end of the story?** For me, the most important stories are those that teach us something. What did you learn from your experience? In writing *Where the Water Meets the Sand*, I realized that many of the lessons I learned in childhood, I later utilized and appreciated as an adult.

# CHAPTER 8:

# Mentors Matter

...........................................

In my lifetime, I've had the privilege of both being mentored by others and being a mentor to others. Because I was fortunate in my early years to have positive relationships with adults who reached out to me, I have tried to give back by mentoring others, both personally and professionally, and passing along some of the most compelling wisdom I gained from my own mentors when I was a young child and a teenager. In my career as an educator and a school principal, I implemented many of the life and relationship lessons I learned from these caring adults in my own life into classrooms and creative projects in the academic institutions where I served.

All of the mentors who spent time with me when I was a child did so because they chose to. They befriended me, shared their compassionate wisdom with me, and spent time with me when I had done nothing to earn the benevolence they offered. Their outreach gave me hope and showed me a blueprint for finding the best in youngsters and adults alike. I will never forget these people, some of whom this chapter honors.

## LESSONS FROM MY GRANDFATHER

I'm named after my grandfather, my mother's father. He was Tira Garland Sexton, and he was a farmer in Brownfield, Texas. We called him PaPa. When Daddy and Mother traveled around the country looking for a doctor who could cure Daddy's heart disease, I often stayed with Nennie and PaPa on their farm. By then, I was seven years old. PaPa's major crop was cotton and he took pride in his straight rows and weeded crops. On special evenings, after he returned from the fields and washed up, we'd go for a walk. One evening I'll never forget, I was crying because Mother and Daddy were out of town again. I was desperately homesick. My brother and I were separated. He was staying at his best friend's house in our hometown, Seminole, forty miles from my grandparents' farm in Brownfield.

After church one Sunday afternoon, PaPa said, "Tyra, come with me. We're going to check the cotton rows in the field across the road and see how the crops are doing."

I dragged my sniffling self out of my grandmother's lap and trailed along behind PaPa as we walked out the back door of the farmhouse and across the red dirt road to the cotton field. PaPa had changed out of his Sunday clothes and put on his overalls. I wore jean shorts and a T-shirt and was barefoot. The hot West Texas sun was cooling off and had begun to move closer to the horizon, although the red dirt between my toes was still warm. It felt good and my sniffles began to dissipate. PaPa tried to console me and reminded me Mother and Daddy would be home in one more week. As PaPa and I walked, he pointed to the plants that were producing.

"See, the cotton's looking good. The rows are straight," he said with pride.

"But PaPa," I exclaimed, "this row ahead of us isn't straight. Why is it so crooked?"

In a sheepish sort of way, he explained, "I plowed it that way."

"Why did you do that?" I demanded. "You said the rows were supposed to be straight."

"There was a mother rabbit's nest there. I plowed around it."

Not able to let go, I pursued the issue. "But PaPa, I thought you said rabbits chewed on the cotton!"

PaPa's voice softened. "Sometimes Tyra, what looks right and seems right ain't always right. The day I plowed this row, it just seemed right to go around. Besides, the nest was almost at the end of the row. I didn't lose much cotton."

I understood that PaPa had shared a lesson with me. On other days, he might have plowed over that nest but that day he didn't. He saved that nest, and I loved PaPa for that. Throughout my life, especially when I was in a position of authority as a teacher and school administrator, there were occasions when I determined consequences for children (and sometimes adults) who had made bad choices. Several times, before I made a decision, I heard PaPa's voice whispering in my ear, *What looks right and seems right ain't always right.*

## STORYTELLING: RED ROVER, RED ROVER, COME OVER

Ida Mae Darling is the person who has had the most profound impact on my mastery of storytelling. Our family moved to Seminole, Texas, next door to Ida Mae and her husband, P.D., when I was just two years old. Their influence began almost as soon as I learned to talk. With no children of their own, Ida Mae and P.D. were like second parents for me and my brother. They loved and supported our family during good times and bad.

I spent a lot of my time at their house during my childhood. Ida Mae had been a teacher, and she was always stretching my mind to think outside the box. She and I played our own special version of Red Rover, Red Rover, the well-known children's game. Our game focused on me acting out a story or a character. When the game began, the two of us walked up to an invisible line we had drawn in the grass and stood on opposite sides of the line facing one another. My job was to act out a character or an action I was performing. Ida Mae's job was to guess the role I was acting out or the story character I represented.

Ida Mae began the same way each time. "Red Rover, Red Rover, let Tyra come over," she'd call. "Remember," she'd remind me, "the rule is you cannot be a character you've already been or act out a role you've done before."

Sometimes I acted out a role such as a schoolteacher writing on the chalkboard, turning to my make-believe class of students, pointing to one as if I was running a class. I made believe I was rocking my baby, depicting the song, "Rock-a-bye Baby," or pretended to be the preacher at the First Baptist Church. In the preacher role I flailed my arms and held my breath until my face turned red like the preacher did when he warned us about going to hell.

Ida Mae sparked my imagination and encouraged creativity. I desperately wanted to please her, so I made sure that I came up with something good each time I went to the invisible line. I'm positive that my love of storytelling was born while playing a child's game with an adult, a teacher at heart. I'll always be grateful to Ida Mae for instilling the love of storytelling in me at such an early age. I have carried that with me throughout my own career as an educator and tried to encourage the children that I taught to tell their own stories, just as Ida Mae had done with me.

Before I left my mother's house in Seminole to be admitted to The Menninger Clinic in Topeka, Kansas, I confided in Ida Mae that I was worried about going to Menninger because I didn't have a wealthy person's wardrobe. Most of the patients there were wealthy; I could never have afforded treatment at Menninger had the air force not paid for it.

Ida Mae and P.D. took me shopping at a high-end dress shop in my hometown. I still remember the navy-blue skirt, matching vest, yellow turtleneck sweater, and dressy slacks that they bought for me.

The night before my intake appointment at The Menninger Clinic, I laid out my new clothes, compliments of Ida Mae and P.D.

As I dressed the next morning, I wondered, *Do these clothes make me look like I fit in? Do I look like a wealthy person?* I checked myself out in the floor-to-ceiling mirror. I stood straighter and looked taller in my new outfit. *Wearing the clothes Ida and P.D. bought me is like having their arms wrapped around me like they've done so many times*, I reminded myself. Besides, Mother always said, "The least you can do is look right and act right."

After Mother left the Clinic, and with the passing of time, my doctor wrote orders for me to join the volleyball activity group led by an activity therapist, as well as art therapy and sewing. By then I was no longer preoccupied with fitting in. I realized making friends and becoming a member of the community totally diminished my obsession to fit in.

Years later, P.D. passed first. Ida Mae remained a cherished and beloved friend until her death several years later. Her extended family invited our family to choose something before the estate sale began to remember P.D. and Ida Mae by. I wondered if the candy dish that sat on their coffee table would be among their treasures. It was. Of all the lovely items on the display tables, that was a priceless treasure. My parents were very strict about making sure my brother and I minded our manners, especially when we visited Ida Mae and P.D. Most days when I visited, after P.D. got home from work at the bank or on Saturdays, they invited me to help myself to a treat from the magnificent candy dish with a lid.

One Saturday, as I visited with the two of them, I noticed they hadn't invited me to help myself to a treat. I continued to visit but privately wondered why they hadn't offered me candy. Finally, in exasperation I blurted out, "What's in that dish? I kinda forgot."

The minute I heard my voice, I wanted to take it back, but my rude words were out. A wide grin spread across P.D.'s face, but Ida Mae, the teacher, said, "Miss Tyra"—she never called me Miss Tyra—"would you care for a piece of candy?"

My face blushed and grew hot. I nodded and gazed down at the floor. Mother and Daddy emphasized good manners constantly, especially at Ida Mae and P.D.'s

"What did you say? Did you say yes?" Ida Mae asked.

"Yes, ma'am," I replied, rubbing my clammy hands together. "I would love to have a piece of candy. Thank you."

"Of course," Ida Mae responded. She removed the lid from the candy dish and held the dish out to me so that I could choose my favorite.

Every so often I catch myself in my study, admiring Ida Mae and P.D.'s magnificent, infamous candy dish, which now enjoys a special place on one of my display shelves. It reminds me of Ida Mae and P.D.'s amazing love for our entire family and the time Ida Mae spent teaching me the value of storytelling in addition to insisting

I remember my manners like a young lady when I visited them. Ida Mae and P.D. weren't blood relatives, but they were family. They didn't have to love us, but they did. They loved us just because. We were blessed to have them as such dear friends, and I will always be thankful for all the love and support they gave to our family.

## CHICKEN LADY

I'll never forget one of my very first mentors from when I was a teenager. She set a strong example for me that I have carried since my time with her. During my eighth-grade year, I began to rebel against Mother's rules and blew off school assignments. I was rude and sullen to my teachers. I started hanging out after school on the steps of my junior high school while I waited for Mother to finish preparing her classroom for the next day. Less than two blocks from the school was a popular hamburger joint. When I had money, I'd walk over and order French fries and a Coke. If I was broke, I'd just sit with the other kids, waiting for my ride.

Every day like clockwork, an old woman who lived alone across the street from the junior high school and two doors down from the corner came outside to feed the chickens that ran loose inside the metal fence around her property. I nicknamed her Chicken Lady.

The other kids and I would make up scary stories about her like the old witch in the story of "Hansel and Gretel." One afternoon, I offered a wager for an order of French fries and a Coke if I went into Chicken Lady's house and stayed for a bit. In an instant, my bet was accepted.

I trembled as I opened the squeaky metal gate and focused my eyes on Chicken Lady's front porch. Her yard was full of weeds up to my knees. Chickens scattered in all directions as I walked into the yard, down the crumbling sidewalk lined with purple irises, and up to the old lady's front porch. As soon as I knocked on the door, it opened a crack. A tiny old lady's face peered out as she dragged out the word *yes* as if it was spelled, "Yees."

"If I come in your house for a few minutes, the kids on the steps of the junior high school will buy me an order of French fries and a Coke," I blurted out.

"Come on in," she replied in a soft voice. "Have a seat."

My brain flashed on the old witch in "Hansel and Gretel" as I followed her into the living room furnished with two high-back burgundy velvet chairs beside a small lamp table that faced an old-fashioned settee upholstered with pink flowered material. As soon as I sat down on the edge of one of the velvet chairs, I introduced myself.

"My name's Tyra Decker," I said in a raspy nervous voice.

"Oh," she replied with a smile, "you must be Cliff Decker's daughter."

"You knew my dad?" My eyes widened. Daddy had died four years earlier, and I still missed him terribly.

"Yes. My husband and I bought a car from him."

When I realized Chicken Lady had known him personally, I was hooked. Knowing that this old lady and her husband had done business with my dad reduced my apprehension. I scooted comfortably back in my chair.

"Would you like some tea and cookies?" she asked.

I nodded and added, "Yes, ma'am, please," as I remembered my manners.

"You can call me Mrs. Martin," she said as she left me sitting in one of the high-back chairs. She returned almost immediately carrying a tray with hot tea served in beautiful china cups and a matching plate heaped with vanilla wafer cookies.

Mrs. Martin continued her story about her husband buying a car from my daddy. She emphasized how much her husband trusted my dad. He'd said Cliff Decker was an honest man and that he wouldn't think of buying a car from anyone else. "My husband's gone now," she finished softly. "It's just me and the chickens."

I drank my tea and ate the vanilla wafers. Then I realized that Mother might be waiting for me at the junior high. "I need to go now," I said, wondering if the kids across the street were thinking I'd been pushed into the oven. I quickly added, "May I come back sometime?" I was curious about what else Mrs. Martin could tell me about Daddy and curious about the old lady in general. I had grandmothers, but even they weren't as old as Mrs. Martin. I guessed she was over ninety years old.

The lesson I learned that day was that what you see is not always what you get. Although taking a chance on Mrs. Martin happened not because of kindness in my heart but rather because of a teenage dare, I knew in that first short visit that I wanted to be her friend.

I visited Mrs. Martin often after school the rest of the year. She told me stories of how her family settled in West Texas and about circuit rider preachers who traveled from community to community, preaching at Sunday services. She told stories of growing up as a little girl on the prairie. I looked forward to the afternoons I could stop by and took small gifts to her.

Mrs. Martin's house was safe. She encouraged me and always had time for me. She was my nonjudgmental oldest friend. In retrospect, I realize she was one of the first adults I confided in as a troubled teenager. She encouraged me to do my best in school and reminded me my daddy would want me to work hard at my studies. She gave me hope and treated me with dignity even though I was a snotty teenager; she didn't believe I was hopeless and ruined just because my grades were failing.

I still had problems after my time with Mrs. Martin, but I held a place in my heart for her. I was always welcome, and she was interested in my schoolwork and in how my mother was doing. She marveled at how brave my mom was to go back to college after Daddy died and become a teacher to support my brother, me and my baby sister, born after Daddy's death. Mrs. Martin reminded me that Mother was striving mightily to take care of our family.

Mrs. Martin didn't have to love me—she wasn't a member of my family, after all—but she did, without ever judging me. She always made me feel safe. I'll never forget her.

When Mrs. Martin died, her niece called my mother and asked if I would like anything from her house to remember her by. I met a good friend of mine, who turned out to be Mrs. Martin's grandnephew. A part of me felt uncomfortable going through Mrs. Martin's things after she was gone, and I didn't see anything I wanted that belonged to Mrs. Martin until we went down to the basement. It was full of treasures. I was delighted when I discovered a stack of old *Saturday Evening Post* magazines. I thumbed through them and chose a 1929 issue. I chose it because it included an extensive interview of Albert Einstein by George Sylvester Viereck entitled, "What Life Means to Einstein." The advertisements included ads about motorcar heaters by the

Metalcraft Company, the Hotel Knickerbocker in Chicago, and Hanes Underwear. Through the years, the 1929 *Post* faded, but my memory of Mrs. Martin never has.

I've had wonderful lifelong examples of how much mentors matter. They change lives and instill hope. I learned so much from Mrs. Martin, and during those difficult teenage years when I felt so misunderstood and was so angry about losing my father, visiting Chicken Lady made me feel useful. She said she looked forward to my visits, and I knew she was one of my true friends, worthy of my trust.

## A TEENAGER WITH ADULT RESPONSIBILITIES

Because of my own behavioral struggles in adolescence, I have always been a passionate supporter of programs serving early teen students. In fact, one of the most important life lessons I learned over five decades of working in academia is that, despite their diversity in terms of ethnicity, religion, or class, teenage kids tend to struggle with similar issues: a need for acceptance, a desire for respect, and an insatiable curiosity about the world and all that's in it.

As a junior high school teacher in Topeka, Kansas, I worked with a student population comprising a rainbow of cultures. One fifteen-year-old student, Felicia, arrived late to school twice during the first nine weeks. School policy dictated that I send students to the office to see the principal after three tardies. I knew that upon receiving her third tardy slip, she'd be required to stay after school. When I asked Felicia why she was late, her only reply was an insolent, defiant shrug. Instead of sending her to the office, I asked her to get her lunch tray from the cafeteria and meet me in my classroom at lunchtime.

As we sat down to eat, I explained to her, once again, the seriousness of her offense. At first, she remained defensive, withdrawn, and sullen, but she finally broke down with a tearful, angry rejoinder: "I have a baby. My mom can't get him to the sitter before school, so it's up to me to bathe and dress him and walk him to the sitter's before I come to school. I just can't get here on time even if I want to. My baby comes first."

My heart dropped into my stomach. How did this fifteen-year-old have the strength, the determination, and the stamina to get herself to school under these circumstances? My better angels took charge, and I immediately decided to work something out. "If you'll come in for lunch every day to make up the time you miss in the morning, we'll eat together and I'll catch you up on what you missed. In return, I expect you to turn in all your work and do your best. Do we have an agreement?" I asked. She nodded, gratitude shining in her eyes.

I admired Felicia's strength of character and could see she was smart enough to learn the lessons she had missed. Despite daunting obstacles, she was doing her best to juggle all of life's responsibilities even at her tender age. After several weeks of lunches together, she began smiling routinely.

When she graduated from eighth grade, she stopped by my room to say good-bye. I told her how proud I was of her, and how convinced I was that she and her baby would do well. She hugged me and thanked me, filled with excitement about going on to high school.

I recalled my own experience as an unwed teenage mother, fortunate enough to find help through a church that had offered me a place to live when I made the difficult decision to give my baby girl up for adoption. As Felicia walked away, I thought, *If only you knew what a gift you've been to me by allowing me to give you a second chance and to give back.*

## GRAND-FRIENDS: SHARING STORIES BRINGS GENERATIONS TOGETHER

Personal relationships with older generations have always impacted my life in strong and positive ways. Over time I've come to realize how transformational and magical those relationships were for my confidence and growth. Perhaps the impact of older adult friends in my own life as a youngster was the impetus for initiating the Grand-Friends Program, a writing project some middle school teachers and I developed for children in one of our sixth-grade English classes when I was director of instruction in Highland Park, Illinois. In order to help our students engage with senior citizens in our community, and to challenge them academically, we designed an opportunity for our students to get to know individuals from a local senior center and gather information for a larger writing project.

We invited individuals from our local senior center to meet our sixth-grade students for a "getting to know you" opportunity. The seniors and their contact at the local senior center were thrilled. Our goals were to give the sixth-grade class the opportunity to build relationships with seniors, person-to-person, through sharing personal stories, help those same students appreciate and understand the benefits of learning about the older generation's experiences, and build new community partnerships.

## OUR FIRST MEETING

The senior center staff had tables set up before we arrived for our first meeting. Seniors were each seated with an empty chair next to them. When we arrived, the children simply chose an empty chair and sat next to the individual who would become their grand-friend for our activity. Maybe because everyone was interested and excited about the opportunity, we never had to change partners for the program. Each match from the first meeting was perfectly made.

Each student-senior team spent twenty to thirty minutes per person learning about each other. Students had been prepped at school during brainstorming sessions on a list of topics they would like to share with their grand-friend senior partner. After meeting their partners during the get to know-you session and listening to their partner's stories, students and seniors picked a story from their partner's repertoire they wanted their partner to write about. They each had a personal investment in wanting to learn and create a good representation of the other's story since, at the final get-together, each grand-friend would tell the group their student's story and each student would tell the group about their grand-friend's story.

Before that next meeting at our school, one of our children's grandparents passed away. The grand-friends and children in the project contacted our school, sharing their desire to attend the funeral so they could rally around the child who had lost his grandparent. We never intended for death to be a topic of discussion for this class, but no one is immune to loss.

Our school counselors met with our students, and our grand-friend seniors and sixth graders sent cards and condolences to the student whose grandmother had died. As a school and a community, we were prepared and had the extra ability to give this student in grief a true nurturing environment. Our discussions and meetings with our grand-friends had laid the groundwork.

## OUR STORY-SHARING FINAL MEETING

We invited our grand-friends to our middle school for a last session and story sharing. Everyone was excited. We videotaped the gathering as each grand-friend and student introduced their respective partner and told their partners' stories. Afterward, the audience had the opportunity to ask questions of either friend. All of our students who participated verified on their evaluation reports that they left with a deeper connection to their community and a good understanding of the commonalities that exist between younger and older generations. The seniors' evaluations were equally positive. According to our students, many of them stayed connected with their grand-friends for years after this initial introduction.

Throughout the grand-friends program, I couldn't help but reminisce about some of the relationships I've discussed earlier in this chapter: my grandfather, Ida Mae and P.D., Chicken Lady (Mrs. Martin), and others. There is a natural kinship between seniors and preadolescent and adolescent children. I believe it stems from students not yet being fully independent while seniors are just beginning to feel a loss of that same independence. It's as if they have a common enemy: lack of autonomy. These cross-generational relationships are so beneficial for communities. Students often react to outside guidance more positively than they do to directives from their parents. Seniors develop a greater sense of self-worth from these friendships too. They are shown how much they are valued and that their stories make a difference in the lives of others.

# YOUR TURN

Many of us remember older teenagers, next-door neighbors, scout leaders, church or synagogue teachers and leaders, or schoolteachers, and on occasion, some of us learned an important lesson from a stranger we never forgot. Recall the adults or older friends who have mentored you. What did you learn from them? Have you mentored children, teenagers, or even adults or seniors who had a particular need, or simply needed a friend or someone to spend time with them? Were there adults in your life who made a difference that you remember with gratitude? Are there important life lessons you learned from an adult or even a child you spent quality time with that you remember fondly? What were the lessons you learned and continue to apply to your life to this day? Even if it was only a one-time event, if you learned an important lesson, consider writing about it.

**What was it like at the beginning of the story?** Include the facts—where you were, when the event took place, who was there, and how you felt.

**What happened?** Write the story like you would tell it verbally. Use active language and give examples. Include as much detail as possible to vividly recreate the scene. Most important, what was the issue? Was there a problem, a tragedy, a celebration?

**What was it like at the end of the story?** For me, the most important stories are those that teach us something. What did you learn from your experience? In writing *Where the Water Meets the Sand*, I realized that many of the lessons I learned in childhood, I later utilized and appreciated as an adult.

# CHAPTER 9:

# Creativity

.............................

The Menninger Clinic was the first place I learned about the power of storytelling to heal and inspire hope. My therapist encouraged me to read my writing aloud during our sessions and told me to keep writing. During the creative process, I experienced "aha" moments, physical and emotional responses that I had not previously recognized or owned. These responses were often amazing and telling; they expanded my self-awareness and gave me new perspective on other people's experiences and emotions. All these years later, writing has brought me to a place of acceptance and peace with specific events, relationships, and places from the past and present.

Writing is only one of many forms of creative self-expression that can enhance our well-being and remind us of people, places, and events that leave an indelible footprint on our soul. I am convinced we are all artists in our hearts. We long to express ourselves and communicate what's important to us. Finding other artistic outlets can help us discover gems of hope, serenity, and gratitude in the hardest of times, and help us celebrate all of life's little triumphs and joys as well. I know I'm not unique in having lovely and sad stories; I encourage you to share yours through any media that speaks to you. What do you love to do? Is it photography, painting, writing, carving, sculpting, gardening, or building birdhouses? Whatever it is, do it! You'll be glad you did.

The first time I remember being proud of something I made was in Miss Talbert's second grade class. She found me crying on the playground after school and invited me in to finger-paint until the school bus came. I painted a black iris. My daddy and mother had traveled to Galveston for Daddy to see his heart specialist. Each time they left, I missed them terribly and I feared I would never see them again. Even though the painting of my iris was black, I didn't think of it as sad at the time since Miss Talbert encouraged me to use black finger-paint. She taught me to smear the entire page with black paint using the palms of my hands. I created the tall iris leaves by starting at the bottom of the page with the sides of my fingers then the palm of my hand and finally pushed the rest of my whole arm onto the paint like a huge brush. That made the leaves wide at the bottom and long, tall and slender at the top. The hairs on my arm created tiny lines on the leaves like the tiny veins on a real iris leaf.

Even though Miss Talbert encouraged us to paint with black, I could have chosen a different color. I chose black paint that day because I was afraid. In my last act of defying the truth, I slapped a red dollop of paint at the top of a tall flower stem made by using my finger-nail in the center of the black plant. *There*, I remember thinking, *just maybe Mother and Daddy will find a cure.* And with that, I felt a grin spread across my face.

I gave the painting to my grandmother Nennie, an interior decorator. Beaming, Nennie put her arm around me and said, "I love it, and I love you. Thank you for making me a gift with your own two hands. I'm going to hang this painting in the hallway for everyone to see. When the irises aren't in bloom, I'll have yours to enjoy and think of all the colors it could be."

Nennie paused and then said, "Tyra, my prayer for you is that someday you will see irises in all the colors of the rainbow. Someday you'll paint irises in greens, purples, reds, and yellows. I love this iris you made for me with black strong leaves and tiny lines etched by the hairs in your arms with a light-gray background. One day, this tiny red flower in the center will grow larger than this whole painting. Until then, this is the best iris I have ever gotten."

Nennie was supportive and loving, but she also had a way of communicating a better way of thinking about things without preaching. She, as much as anyone, knew how homesick I felt when Mother and Daddy went searching for a doctor to cure Daddy. Everyone including me knew Daddy was really ill. All the grown-ups whispered about Daddy's illness like I wasn't around, but I heard them and I knew. Each time Mother and Daddy left, I had nightmares they wouldn't come home.

When I was at The Menninger Clinic, art therapy was an integral part of the inpatient program. I skipped the first couple of required art therapy classes. Dr. Roberts had scheduled them to begin right after I arrived at the Clinic, but I spent most of those first days in bed with the covers pulled up over my face. I hated waking up to the horrible feeling of impending doom that followed me around like a ghost. My clinical depression meant that I simply did not want to face the day or deal with other people.

On the third day, Dr. Roberts knocked on my door and announced he was there to escort me to art therapy. "Art therapy is important," he said. "It gets you up and out of bed. It gives you an opportunity to express yourself and be around other people without having to interact with them if you choose to focus on your art project." I rolled my eyes but nodded at the same time.

As we walked to the activity building, Dr. Roberts explained that I'd have sewing each day, followed by art therapy. He introduced me to Mona the sewing instructor and then Kyle the art therapist. Dr. Roberts reminded me he would see me at three, our regular appointment time, in my room.

That morning Mona introduced me to the other patients and showed me three rolls of fabric I could choose from. I picked striped material. Mother always said, "Stripes make us look thinner." Because I felt fat all the time, I thought, *If stripes really can make me look thinner, this fabric is the obvious choice.*

After sewing, I took my time strolling over to art therapy. Kyle showed me around the art shop and pointed out the project options, including painting, drawing, making jewelry, and sculpting. I chose sculpting because it reminded me of how much fun I'd had using Play-Doh back in 1956, when it was all the rage. I'd found it much easier to work with than the clay we used at school. The challenge for me was that I'd tried to sculpt my black cocker spaniel, Princess. I did not have the patience, talent, or ability to create Princess's likeness. Her face looked like a pig's. So I'd decided to roll out the Play-Doh with Mother's rolling pin and use her numerical cookie cutters to make something recognizable. Once I had success with the cookie cutters, I created fruit: apples, bananas, and grapes. Mother had a picture of fruit in a cornucopia in the kitchen. I decided to sculpt a cornucopia out of Play-Doh too and placed the fruit inside. It wasn't a masterpiece, to say the least, but it was a start.

In art therapy at Menninger, I spent the first several classes rolling clay into a ball and then flattening it with the palm of my hand until it was as flat as a pancake. Then I rolled the pancake into a ball and repeated the process. I loved how the clay felt in my hands and spent several days of art therapy doing just that.

I told Kyle that I had decided to sculpt my left hand with clay. He said sculping clay was a great idea and told me about the famous French sculptor Rodin and how he was famous for his sculptures of hands. I especially liked his sculptures *The Cathedral* and *The Hand of God*. I spent several more days stretching the clay, rolling it into a lopsided oval across the table but catching it before it fell and squashed on the floor. Working the clay took me on a journey through childhood memories, good times and bad times, and reminded me that memories are stories my soul felt were worth storing away, lessons that mattered. It was relaxing, prayerful, and calming and gave me hope that I could get better. It increased my determination to get well, rather than to fight the therapy.

In 2017, I returned to the creative experience of sculpting and decided to create another hand. I have always loved hands. As a small child, the image of God's hands was prevalent in the books given to us at the beginning of each term in our Sunday school classes. Our hands reveal so much about us: our age, our race, and, for some, the kind of work we do.

PaPa, my mother's father, had hands that were large, strong, ruddy, and gnarled from farming—working the soil, raising cotton and maize in addition to maintaining a large peach orchard and acres of corn, green beans, and black-eyed peas for our extended family—but, at the same time, gentle and loving when he prayed and played with his grandchildren. When my father died of a heart attack at the age of thirty-six, I was nine years old. Patting and holding Daddy's hands as he laid in his open casket is a memory seared in my mind forever.

One of my favorite photos of Laura, my daughter, is of her exuberantly clapping her hands with delight as her father, Larry, sat on the floor, legs crossed, playing a game of patty-cake. In Western cultures, it's acceptable to touch one another by shaking hands with friends as well as strangers. In many ways, we talk with our hands and telegraph our openness through our gestures and willingness to physically reach out to one another.

Returning to sculpting recently after forty years has been a delight, a return to a former muse and a soothing, calming movement in which my hands make a happy or sad memory tangible by smoothing, pinching, forming, and caressing a lump of clay. My left hand was my model as I molded the clay with my right hand. Completing my first bronzed sculpted hand has been an amazing celebration of beautiful memories of the loving, committed hands in my life. While I was sculpting, there were times I emitted an unplanned sound of joy and approval from my throat. *Where did that come from?* I realized, for the first time in a long time, that I had just done something that made me feel truly proud. These were quiet but audible giggles that slid out of my mouth almost like an infant's expression of delight.

The inspiration for my next sculpting project is Rafa, a young guitarist who volunteered at MD Anderson. Stepping out of the elevator at MD Anderson on a regular checkup, I scanned the familiar huge main lobby, noticing that the children's art project volunteers were selling Christmas Cards, aprons, yard decorations, and other small items made from the artistic designs created by pediatric patients at the hospital.

While shopping for Christmas cards, I realized someone was playing beautiful guitar music. I followed the music and was drawn to a young man playing his instrument. His beautiful music, the movement of his hands on the guitar strings, and his gorgeous smile captivated me as I stood listening until he finished his piece.

"Your music is beautiful. What's your name?" I inquired.

"I'm Rafa," he said, smiling.

"Your music is beautiful!" I gushed. "May I take a photo of your hands?"

Blushing, he flashed a wide grin. "Yes, of course."

I added, "May I post it on Facebook and on my website? Are you a volunteer?"

"Yes, yes, and yes," he responded, still beaming his beautiful smile.

Because of Rafa's inspiration, I am currently sculpting hands playing the guitar. It's more difficult than the fisted hand named *Determination* that I wrote about earlier in this piece, but that's part of the challenge. I find delving into something new or more difficult than the last project instills me with excitement and reward when I am finished. Perhaps it keeps me young.

For me, creating something with my hands is soothing and calming, though frustrating at times. The frustration provokes me to find a solution to a problem I'm having with my sculpture, often by accident.

Before we said good-bye, I asked if Rafa would like the address of my website and, because he was such a gentleman, he said yes.

"What's your website about?" he asked.

"My book, *Where the Water Meets the Sand*, focuses on fighting the stigma against people with mental illness . . ." I replied as I began my spiel. Gracious and kind, he seemed interested.

My encounter with Rafa was a highlight at the beginning of my odyssey that day. He was a kind young man donating his talent, time, and goodwill to strangers. When we focus exclusively on negativity, we often overlook the happiness that surrounds us. When we create a sculpture, play a musical instrument, write a poem or a book, or create a painting, we express our innermost feelings: joy or sadness, appreciation or disdain, love or hate, beauty or ugliness.

## THE BIG EASY

I find New Orleans to be one of America's most iconic destinations, a unique mélange of distinct cultures, languages, flavors, and smells, and a place where the discordant sounds of jazz, blues, early African, Caribbean, Creole, and zydeco music can be heard simultaneously from nearly every quarter.

In June 2018, I had the pleasure of visiting the Big Easy while attending a conference organized by the Independent Book Publishing Association at the American Libraries Association. The IBPA is a favorite organization of mine because it supports independent publishers and writers like me.

Saturday afternoon I took some time off from the conference and headed down to the iconic Café Du Monde, located in the world-famous French Quarter, where patrons have satiated themselves on steaming café au lait, chicory coffee, and sumptuous, powdered sugar–dusted beignets since 1862. While the beignets and chicory coffee were what first attracted me, I was quickly caught up in watching a gathering crowd by the park at Jackson Square, an excellent vantage point from which to take in the sights and sounds of this unique and timeless place.

As I strolled around the square enjoying the view of St. Louis Cathedral, the oldest cathedral in what would ultimately become the United States, I was drawn to the hypnotic sound of two street musicians playing drums nearby. One of them especially caught my eye as he sat on a park bench drumming in perfect rhythm. He paused for a few minutes to rest, leaving his partner to carry on the rhythmic beat solo. I pushed forward, approached him, and introduced myself, asking if I could join him on the bench for a few minutes. He graciously assented, and we began to chat.

"My name's Tyra," I said, sitting down. "What's yours?"

"David, ma'am. Where're you from?"

"These days, Texas," I responded, "but Chicago is my second home."

"Really," David responded. "I grew up in Chicago and my mom was an elementary school teacher there. I believe she taught at Ryerson Elementary School, but I think it's closed now," he reflected, a bit wistfully.

"Really," I said. "I was a school administrator in a couple of Chicago towns called Highland Park and River Forest, next to Oak Park."

David grinned in recognition. "I know Oak Park. Nice place."

Suddenly, catching some invisible cue, he jumped up, mumbling, "I got to jump back into the piece in just a minute."

"Would you mind if I take some photos of your hands while you drum, David?" I asked. "One of my hobbies is sculpting—especially hands."

"No problem," he said. "Hey, would you like to stay and play for a few minutes?" he asked, gesturing toward his drum.

"No, I just want to take some pictures of you playing." I noted self-consciously that the throng of onlookers had grown while we spoke.

Then, in a seemingly effortless manner, he resumed his drumming in perfect sync with his partner and with the universe. I took some photos and listened for a while. As the afternoon sun began to fade, I waved good-bye and walked off. David nodded back, as if to acknowledge our shared experience as two strangers who briefly made a human connection.

As I headed back to the conference, I was struck by how much David and I shared, despite all our differences. As I reflected, David and I had very little in common. We were separated by race, age, gender, lifestyle, and education, and yet we were still able to relate to each other for a moment by celebrating our common humanity and the things we shared—Chicago, the education profession, and a passion for music.

My brief but memorable connection with David was an example of why I keep encouraging you to share your own stories: humans can connect to each other in meaningful ways when they invite others into the intricate tapestries of their lives.

I'm thrilled to have rediscovered that sculpting is a vehicle for storytelling. After I finish the sculpture of Rafa's hands playing the guitar, a sculpture of David's hands playing his drums will be next. Sculpting is the visual art that resonates most with me, but any kind of art form can inspire a great story: photography, drawing, woodworking, ceramics, floral arranging, or cooking, for example. The trick is to find what brings you alive and makes you want to write about it, although the very act of creating other art forms can also tell stories through their own special mediums.

# YOUR TURN

......................................................

Many of us remember working with tempura paint, finger painting, cutting shapes out of construction paper for bulletin boards, and making construction paper chains, clay models, and dioramas, especially in Sunday school, elementary and middle school, and even in high school. As parents and grandparents, we often entertain youngsters under our care with art projects. Even as adults, many of us enjoy creating scrapbooks filled with personal family photographs of celebrations, awards earned by family members, and special holidays such as shower and wedding invitations, photographs of special family events during the holidays and birthday celebrations, as well as newspaper articles celebrating family members' accomplishments.

In my ongoing quest to find my own fulfilling creative pursuits, I have found that, besides writing books, other forms of creativity, such as sculpting, painting, cooking (barbecued brisket is my specialty), exploring music, gardening, and attending concerts pique my inward desire to create. The bottom line is, whatever you love to do, do it. It will arouse your desire to create and support your sense of accomplishment.

**Describe specific examples of unforgettable art projects that you and your family members or friends have created, as well as any fond memories or stories those art projects inspired. What was it like at the beginning of the story?** Include the facts—where you were, when the event took place, who was there, and how you felt.

**What happened?** Write the story like you would tell it verbally. Use active language and give examples. Include as much detail as possible to vividly recreate the scene. Most important, what was the issue? Was there a problem, a tragedy, a celebration?

**What was it like at the end of the story?** For me, the most important stories are those that teach us something. What did you learn from your experience? In writing *Where the Water Meets the Sand*, I realized that many of the lessons I learned in childhood, I later utilized and appreciated as an adult.

# CHAPTER 10:

# Spirituality

..............................

Contemplating the subject of spirituality can feel uncomfortable, given that each of us comes to understand and define the concept in our own way. My own perspective is based on a lifetime of trying to understand the "still, small voice" that helps guide my behavior. For me, spirituality manifests itself when I become aware of that inner voice, tugging at my heart in circumstances in which I face a moral choice. The minute I feel myself contemplating going down a wrong path, I feel physically anxious or even get a lump in my throat at the prospect of taking actions that might be hurtful to myself or another. I believe this internal voice acts as a compass, helping to guide my soul along life's convoluted path and helping me to meet life's challenges head on.

In developing a sense of spirituality as adults, we frequently find ourselves looking back on our experience with religion; the dos and don'ts and the church rituals that were often so embedded in our childhood years.

My family was Southern Baptist and we attended the First Baptist Church in our hometown. My mother taught Sunday school classes and made sure we attended Sunday school and church on Sunday mornings and Training Union on Sunday night before church services with the adults. Training Union was like Sunday school. In Training Union, we had sword drills before our Bible lesson. We'd stand in a circle, holding our Bibles in front of us as the teacher called out a Bible verse. When the teacher said, "Go," we'd rush to the find the Bible verse. The first one to find the verse would step forward in the circle and the teacher would call on them to read the passage. I practiced for sword drills at home. I wanted to be first and I wanted to win.

I always memorized the Bible verse for our children's Sunday school lesson, which was held on Sunday morning before the church service with grown-ups. That's where I got comfortable speaking in front of a group.

One of my favorite biblical stories was the tale of Moses. I loved the drama of Pharaoh's daughter discovering the baby floating in a hidden basket among the bulrushes and choosing to adopt him as her own. Moses's older sister, Miriam, observed the encounter and offered to find a Hebrew woman to nurse the baby, who turned out to be his own mother. It was all part of an elaborate and clever ruse on the part of the parents to save Moses's life following an edict from Pharaoh ordering the slaughter of all newborn male Hebrew children. Many years later Moses went on to deliver the Israelites out of bondage into the Promised Land.

When I was an unwed teenage mother, I also made the decision to give up my baby girl to another family. I chose not to see or hold my daughter after the birth because I was afraid I would change my mind and it would be too hard to give her up. Over my life, I mourned her loss and felt guilty that I'd abandoned her, but I found solace in the story of Moses and how his family had given him up to save his life. I prayed to God that like Moses, my baby girl would be loved and special. I still think of her and am comforted that I did the right thing for her and for me.

The story of Joseph was another favorite Bible story. Joseph's jealous brothers sold him to merchants and painted his coat with goat's blood after their father, who loved Joseph best, had given him his famous coat of many colors. Joseph's brothers took his bloody coat to their father and told him that Joseph had been killed.

Joseph was jailed but ultimately became an important figure in Pharaoh's court because of his ability to interpret dreams. Joseph was promoted to be chief administrator of Egypt after interpreting Pharaoh's dreams that there would be seven years of outstanding crops followed by seven years of famine.

Because of the shortage of food, Joseph's brothers traveled to Egypt to buy grain. A second time, the sons' father, Jacob, sent his sons back to Egypt to buy more grain. This time, the brothers brought the youngest son, Benjamin. Joseph hid a silver cup in Benjamin's sack and then accused Benjamin of being a thief. When one of the older brothers pleaded to stay in Benjamin's place, Joseph realized that the character of his brothers had changed and invited them to eat supper at his house. At that point, Joseph told his brothers he was their brother, Joseph, whom they had sold into bondage. His brothers were afraid because of their deceitful behavior toward him and because of his position of power in Egypt. Rather than punish his brothers, Joseph told them that he had forgiven them because everything that happened was God's plan. He told his brothers to bring their father to Egypt and invited his whole family to move to Egypt, where they would be together and they would have all the food they needed. Jacob was thrilled that Joseph was alive and grateful to have his entire family together.

I learned from Joseph's story to never hold back forgiveness even though it may be hard. There are times I have to pray for forgiveness for myself because I am having so much trouble forgiving. When I was a young child, Mother and Daddy traveled looking for a cure for Daddy's heart trouble. My brother and I were left with relatives or friends. I worried I'd never see my parents again. I was seven and it was the first time I remember being afraid. Some days, I couldn't understand why they had to leave. We had a wonderful doctor in our hometown, and when Daddy got sick, he could go to the hospital there.

When I wasn't afraid, I was mad. Mad at God who the preacher said could fix anything. The preacher said God could perform miracles and that meant make everything better. But God didn't give Daddy a miracle and I couldn't understand why. There were times I was furious with God and wondered whether, if I was a better servant of God's, he would cure Daddy. My brother acted like he was the grown-up when my parents were gone. He tried to tell me what to do.

*You're not a grown-up*, I'd mumble. *You're not in charge of me.*

If my aunt and uncle were staying with us, I'd hide in the closet in the dark and pray my heart out to God to bring Mother and Daddy home. Some days, I'd say awful things to God like, *If you're so great, why can't you make Daddy well?* I'd challenge God through my tears. Then I'd remember Joseph. *Maybe God would make it better for Daddy and our family. Maybe we'd all get back together, like Joseph's family. God, let us be like Joseph's family and be together again*, I'd plead until I fell asleep on the closet floor.

Almost everyone I knew in my hometown were Protestants—Baptist, Methodist, Church of Christ, and Presbyterian. One of my best friends was Catholic and another close friend, Ellen, was Jewish. Her family owned a dry-goods store in town. One day, I heard Mother and her close friend discussing how awful it was for Ellen's parents to keep their store open on Sundays, giving Mexicans, who worked on local farms bringing in the harvest or moving irrigation pipe, a place to shop when they came to town on their day off.

After overhearing Mother and her friend commenting about Ellen's parents' store being open on Sunday, I asked my friend why her parents opened their store on Sunday. She explained that the Jewish Sabbath was on Saturday. I'd never heard of such a thing, but I was curious and asked her to tell me about her family's faith. I was amazed that she knew the stories about Moses and Joseph, just not about Jesus in the New Testament. I wondered why it wasn't okay for Ellen to worship God the way her family chose. That's when I learned that other people had different religions and faiths. I knew our dear friends Ida Mae and P.D. went to the Methodist church and I had friends who went to the Presbyterian church and also to the Church of Christ, but Ellen was the only friend I had whose family worshiped on Saturday. Then I remembered from school that our country's constitution says we have the freedom to worship as we choose, and I felt better.

When Larry and I married in 1966, I was nineteen and he was twenty. We joined the First Baptist Church in Lubbock, Texas. Whenever I worried aloud about having enough money to finish college and pay the bills, Larry would say, "Tyra, you always say the Bible says, 'It came to pass.' Don't hang on to what you fear might happen. I think 'it came to pass' means, 'don't worry, let it pass on through.'"

Larry's family did not go to church, but he demonstrated more hope and faith than I did. He had a calmness about him that everything would be fine. Over time, I started to feel safe because of his example. "Promise me you'll give faith a chance," he'd say. But four years later, he was on his way to Vietnam and I was more afraid of losing him than ever.

After Larry was killed in the war and Laura and I moved to the trailer home he had purchased for us in Topeka, we began attending an American Baptist Church. On weekends, Laura and I would take a picnic basket out to Lake Shawnee. I'd grown up in arid West Texas and the lake was like a foreign place to me. Before eating our picnic lunch, I'd take Laura wading at the edge of the lake and marvel that though I didn't have Larry, I had our daughter.

The trees, the lake, the families picnicking, and the fun of my two-year-old daughter gave me a purpose, hope, and a belief that our world would get better. I felt like Larry's spirit was there with us at the lake. It reminded me of the three of us, Larry, Laura, and me playing at Fort Walton Beach in Florida when Larry was in pilot training on the plane he would fly in Vietnam.

Part of trying to rebuild my life after Larry's death was finally admitting to myself that I was an alcoholic. In 1981, I joined a support group to help me stop drinking. This group helped me face the reality that my life was in shambles when it came to my faith. With support from my fellow alcoholics, I revisited the Serenity Prayer first taught to me by my grandmother Nennie when I was a teenager:

> *God grant me the serenity to accept the things I cannot change*
> *The courage to change the things I can*
> *And the wisdom to know the difference.*

The group taught me and others to understand that God meant God as I understand God. They taught me to use the group to lean on until I could reunite with the God of my understanding, and if I couldn't, to use the group as my higher power.

During this time, I began researching the religions and faiths of the world to better understand what God meant to me and to others. I had grown up following the Christian tradition and I started there. As a child, I joined the First Baptist Church and accepted Christ. But what about other people, who live in other countries, and learn a different religion? When I moved to Highland Park, Illinois, to work in School District 108, the community was about 60 percent Jewish. The community and board of education, the teachers and friends I met there, embraced me. I was thrilled and felt I had an inkling of how my little friend Ellen may have felt in my hometown since her family was the only Jewish family.

Although there were Protestant churches in Highland Park and I attended one of them, I also learned so much from my Jewish colleagues and friends in Highland Park. I learned their text is the Torah, the Hebrew Bible. I went to synagogue with them and attended Jewish funerals, as well as bar mitzvahs and bat mitzvahs—beautiful coming-of-age ceremonies that symbolized that the children's parents were no longer responsible for their actions but the children were responsible for Jewish ritual law, their ethics and their traditions. Other major religions that I researched during that period were Islam, Buddhism, Hinduism, and Sikhism.

Despite all my curiosity about different faiths and my belief that freedom of religion is a cornerstone of human liberty, I do not consider myself an expert on religion. I've spent a lifetime trying to understand spirituality, and, after slogging through all the impressive words I could write on the subject, the main thing I can tell you is this: I don't believe God, as I understand God, cares what church door we enter or whether we go to a support group for recovering alcoholics who are there for themselves but also to sponsor and give newcomers hope, one day at a time.

God as I understand God made this beautiful planet we call Earth and would never have made so many kinds of beautiful trees if every living thing or person were expected to walk the same walk or take the same path. Can you imagine a world with only fir trees, no pines, evergreens, oaks, and redwoods? In something as important as our faith, our substance of life, I think God has provided a beautiful mosaic of colors and countless roads to travel for a reason. If God wanted us to all worship alike, don't you wonder why God didn't create us all one color, in one place, with one belief system? Do you really think God expects us to all look alike, act alike, and worship in the same way, named by only one religion?

Whatever book you read to learn about God, or whatever way you worship, do things that make you feel reverent. Sing out loud. Dance. Stand by the ocean and smell the salt and laugh as the waves wash up on the shore and spray your face. Live as if today is your last day, and if you wake up the next day, say thank you and do it all over again. Don't lose your hunger to know more and experience as much as you can.

# YOUR TURN

One of my favorite books, *The Spirituality of Imperfection: Storytelling and the Search for Meaning* by Ernest Kurtz and Katherine Ketcham, reminds us of our common struggles, fears, and aspirations through storytelling. It is one of the most powerful modern spiritual books I have read. Write about a time in your life when you have struggled with your own faith or wondered if God has abandoned you. Use these guidelines to tell your story.

**What was it like at the beginning of the story?** Include the facts—where you were, when the event took place, who was there, and how you felt.

**What happened?** Write the story like you would tell it verbally. Use active language and give examples. Include as much detail as possible to vividly recreate the scene. Most important, what was the issue? Was there a problem, a tragedy, a celebration?

**What was it like at the end of the story?** For me, the most important stories are those that teach us something. What did you learn from your experience? In writing *Where the Water Meets the Sand*, I realized that many of the lessons I learned in childhood, I later utilized and appreciated as an adult.

# CHAPTER 11:

# Letting Go

...............................

When I was eight years old, one trait I wanted to have to ensure that I could accomplish my goals and be successful in school was willpower. I am not suggesting I understood what the word *willpower* meant at the time—it's just that in retrospect, I recognized it as a quality I knew I wanted to possess back then. As a third grader, I believed that if I studied hard at school and followed the rules, I would be well liked and, more importantly, my mother and my father would be proud of me. I especially wanted Daddy to be proud of me; after all, I was his little girl and my brother was Mother's big boy. Anyway, that's what they always said.

Sadly, a year later, Daddy died of heart disease. Soon after that I made up my mind to do my best so Daddy would be proud of me in heaven. The problem was that I was sad after his death. I disliked going to school and worried about leaving my baby sister, born two months after Daddy died, alone with a babysitter we didn't know so Mother could go to work as the telephone operator at Seminole Public Schools.

Because I hated leaving the baby alone with a stranger, I pretended to be sick a number of times so I could stay home from school. *I'm sure Daddy would want me to make sure she's safe. If only God hadn't taken him away, Mother wouldn't have to go to work*, I fumed. In retrospect, I realize that appointing myself to keep our baby safe from strangers must have given me a sense of meaning and position in our family after Daddy's death.

At the beginning of my fifth-grade year, searching for a way to stand out was my modus operandi. My teacher's husband, Mr. Lacey, had worked for my dad at McAdoo's Chevrolet and Oldsmobile Dealership. At the beginning of the school year, Mrs. Lacey made a point of expressing her condolences—in front of my class. She mentioned how much her husband missed my dad and said how sorry they both were about his passing. "It's so wonderful that Dorothy"—my mother—"was offered a job as the telephone operator for the school district," she added.

When she'd make these comments in front of the other students, I'd stare at my feet and say nothing as if she hadn't spoken to me, until she finally stopped talking. Rather than making me feel special, the comments made me feel different, like someone to feel sorry for. I reacted by acting as if I didn't hear her when she called on me during class, or by talking to other students when the teacher was giving a lesson. Even if I did respond to Mrs. Lacey's questions, I spoke to her in a smart-aleck tone. I also made up crude songs about her and taught the words to a few of my classmates.

Before Daddy's death I was a good student, made excellent grades, and helped other students with their schoolwork. Now, in my anger, I began to do poorly on my schoolwork. I wanted the world to know I was mad—mad about losing Daddy, mad that Mother had to go to work, and mad about all the things in my life that changed when Daddy died.

My sixth-grade year started off on a disappointing note as well. By then, it had become clear to me that my baby sister was well loved and I wasn't her protector, nor the only one who loved her dearly. A dear friend of our family had offered to babysit my little sister. There was no question she was in good hands. We all doted on her—my mother, my brother, and I, as well as the babysitter and our extended family members. Since I had made it my personal responsibility to watch over her, I felt lost at this new loss of responsibility and sought to find a new niche.

I found the new sense of purpose I craved in my sixth-grade teacher, Mr.

Turnball, a man whom all of us students admired. I was particularly infatuated with him because, for a fatherless child like me, he was a much-needed authority figure, as well as the first male teacher I had ever had. We knew he cared about us because he walked down the aisles to see how we were all doing as we worked on assignments. He taught us all to play chess and organized chess tournaments during recess. As a result, a large number of us purchased inexpensive chess sets in attempts to impress and please him. I loved that Mr. Turnball took an interest in all of us and never played favorites. I made up my mind always to do my best for him.

Years later as a middle school principal and even as superintendent, I organized chess clubs along with teacher coaches for our students who were interested in learning chess or already played. We held chess matches within individual schools. The student who was deemed the best chess player played me in a chess game. I remember being beaten by young adolescents or a bright elementary student on several occasions. Had it not been for Mr. Turnball, I doubt that I would have learned to play chess, let alone had an avenue to get to know a wide variety of chess opponents and the audiences who watched us play.

Once I had determined to try my hardest for Mr. Turnball, I recall studying nonstop for an upcoming major test, on which I earned an almost perfect score, as did the smartest boy in the class. When my fellow students accused me of cheating (although my teacher put a stop to the chatter), my attitude was, *It doesn't matter what I do, I will constantly be accused of wrongdoing.* My will to overcome my status as an academic failure gave way to self-pity and anger. *It's not fair*, I thought. I realized my previous behavior and lack of doing my best in school had resulted in my counterparts seeing me as a failure. Even as an eleven-year-old, I realized I could not shake people's perception that I was a poor student.

That was my first indication that willpower was not the magical trait I hoped it would be. Still, I wasn't ready to give up on it altogether, and I had another chance to test it out when I was fourteen.

By that time, I was in high school. I had become overweight, or at least I thought I was. My brother called me Fats, and at that young age, I didn't understand that older siblings often mercilessly tease their younger siblings. At the time, my brother's teasing was the impetus for me to do something about my weight. I determined I was going to lose weight so I wasn't called Fats again. *I'll show you*, I decided privately.

Not long after making that decision, I bought a purse-size low-carbohydrate diet paperback book on a rack in the local grocery store by the checkout stand. The book included foods you could eat on the low-carb diet and listed the total number of carbohydrates and the portion size a person could eat of each food in one day to lose weight. I'll forever remember the number of carbs I could eat on the diet per day. It was sixty. I lost forty pounds during my freshman year. I was sure if only I could lose weight and be thin, my brother and I would get along better and I would be more likable.

Some of my friends and my teachers commented on my weight loss. "Did you want to lose weight?" they asked. "Are you sick?"

"Oh, no, I'm not sick," I said. "I wanted to lose weight because I look better in my clothes. I've thought I was too heavy for a long time." What I did not say was, *I want my brother to be proud of me*, or *I thought I would be more popular if I were thinner*.

Since I had lost so much weight, my clothes were too large for me. Although Mother usually made my clothes, my grandmother Nennie decided she wanted to treat me to some new outfits, and she took Mother and me on a shopping trip to Hemphill Wells and Dunlap's in Lubbock, Texas, eighty miles north of my hometown. Although I had been sure that being thinner meant I would be more popular at school, I don't recall that my new clothes changed anything in terms of my popularity except that I felt proud, like I was in "high cotton," a West Texas phrase meaning well off, or someone with money.

Although my use of willpower as a child had temporary positive results—the shopping trip for a new outfit with my mom and Nennie when I lost forty pounds, and earning one of the best grades in Mr. Turnball's sixth-grade classroom on an important test—the older I got, the more I realized that these results were not long-lasting and did not ultimately make me feel stronger or better about myself. That's when I began to focus instead on the power of letting go, surrendering to outcomes, one day at a time, rather than muscling through.

Earlier in this book, in the chapter entitled "Just Lock Me Up," I told the story of the first time I learned about the concept of letting go, when my uncle Sonny gave me a horseback-riding lesson and taught me that there are times in life, even if you have an important goal you want to accomplish, when you have to just let go of a certain plan of action if it isn't working out. Numerous times throughout my life, I've heard Uncle Sonny's voice advising me, "Let go of the rope or you're going to get dragged through the shit!"

The importance of letting go of people, places, and things that no longer benefit me was a lesson I learned even more about in the support groups I attended when I got sober. I perceive letting go and willpower as inherently contradictory concepts. In my case, depending on willpower has not proven helpful. I now interpret willpower as meaning that I will determine never to do something again—whether that's something that has become a habit, something I do without thinking (veering off my budget or losing my temper with someone), or an addiction, such as smoking or drinking alcohol. The problem with the word *never* is that it extends from today until my death. I don't do well with that. Never is forever. It feels like a dare, a mocking voice inside my soul that taunts me as if I have thrown down a personal gauntlet. *Really, Tyra? Never ever. Really?*

Promising myself or another person that I will *never* do a particular thing or go to a particular place or be with a particular person is a setup because, in my experience, I can manage only one day at a time. I cannot say, today, "I will *never* do X," but I *can* say, "I will never do X *today*." If I promise myself that there is something I will never do and I then break that promise, I have set myself up for failure. But if I follow my own healthy inner voice one day at a time and I end up breaking that promise, I know that the next day is a new day and a new start. There is hope in one day at a time. It is better than possible—it is doable. For example, a few of my dear friends who are addicted to alcohol have slipped and taken a drink, even though they had made a  decision not to drink alcohol again, one day at a time. However, with support from other recovering alcoholics, we know they can start over in the now or begin a new day tomorrow. This concept of "one day at a time" allows us to let go of the mistakes we've made on all the days before today, and even on the day we're living now, and, in doing so, move forward into a more hopeful future.

Another term for "letting go" is "acceptance." Letting go of any expectation that a day is going to go a particular way also means accepting that that day may proceed differently, and accepting that we must find the tools to face that day whether things are going our way or not. We all get to a place where we think we cannot go on and we think we can't cope. Really, we're just looking through the lenses of loss, sadness, disappointment, and any other word that describes the state of losing hope. The truth is, we *can* cope, and we *can* find hope again, if we accept the concept of doing things one day at a time. The daily mantra I use to remind myself of this is the Serenity Prayer, which I learned in my support group when I got sober, and which I say aloud five times in the morning and five times before I go to bed.

The support group literature also had a slogan: "Let go and let God." Over the years, I've found that letting go of disappointments and hurts has gotten easier than dragging them around with me. The older I get, the easier it is to let go. I am better at listening to others' points of view. It's easier for me to forgive others, as well as myself. Getting more confident in letting go and letting God has made all the difference to my well-being and in my relationships.

Throughout my life, like everyone else, I have had major losses, terrible fears about things that are yet to become a reality, and setbacks. With the help of professionals, I have overcome losing my father when I was a small child, giving my daughter up for adoption when I was a teenager, clinical depression, the tragic death of my soulmate Larry during the Vietnam War, a catastrophic car accident, and alcoholism, bulimia, and cutting. None of those challenges were easy to overcome, but by accepting the truth of them and asking God for the ability to accept the things I cannot change, I made it through. The bottom line is, letting go of old hurts, resentments, and disappointments opens Life's door to a new freedom, a sense of peace and serenity. There are so many people and things to enjoy and learn about regardless of our age. Spending our time and energy with people we enjoy and reaching out to make a difference works for me. Maybe it will work for you, too.

# YOUR TURN

..................................................

Letting go can mean something different to each of us. In my case, letting go of a relationship or a home is very different from letting go of a physical thing. Letting go of a home by moving from one town or state to pursue a new career opportunity has always been hard for me, although I have done it several times. Even as an adult, I've suffered homesickness and a sense of loss whenever I've said good-bye to colleagues and dear friends. However, I've learned that accepting the change, putting one foot in front of the other, and focusing on the new opportunity and environment can be exhilarating. It doesn't mean you don't treasure your former coworkers and friends, or the comfortable day-to-day routine you'd come to love, any less. This perspective has allowed me to have careers in four states and still have close friends and wonderful memories from each place.

Write about a time in your own life when you have had to let go of a relationship or a job or made a physical move. Was it your choice to let go, or someone else's? Did each instance of letting go take you out of your comfort zone? Be sure to share what you've learned from the act of letting go if you think it would encourage others. Use these guidelines to tell your story.

**What was it like at the beginning of the story?** Include the facts—where you were, when the event took place, who was there, and how you felt.

**What happened?** Write the story like you would tell it verbally. Use active language and give examples. Include as much detail as possible to vividly recreate the scene. Most important, what was the issue? Was there a problem, a tragedy, a celebration?

**What was it like at the end of the story?** For me, the most important stories are those that teach us something. What did you learn from your experience? In writing *Where the Water Meets the Sand*, I realized that many of the lessons I learned in childhood, I later utilized and appreciated as an adult.

# CHAPTER 12:

# Breaking Bread

...............................................

Memories of special times often include recollections of food—images of loved ones sharing beautiful meals together and telling stories, images of places where we've enjoyed the local cuisine for the first time, or the preparation of favorite family recipes passed on from one generation to the next. The loveliest thing about cooking food for and sharing it with others is that it's a time to share personal stories together—stories that live on even after those who shared those recipes and memories have passed.

My memories of Christmas, Thanksgiving, and New Year's are peppered with the food my extended family served when we all came together during my childhood. We spent every Christmas Eve at my maternal grandparents' farmhouse, where we shot off firecrackers and gathered in front of the tree while we waited for Santa.

As I grew older, I realized shooting off firecrackers the night of Santa Claus's arrival wasn't as important as the camaraderie my family members shared. I once read that traditions are innovations that stick. Breaking bread with family and enjoying the same traditions year after year instilled in us a fierce commitment to rituals.

On Christmas Day, dinner was served at noon or early afternoon. It included turkey and dressing, giblet gravy, ham, sweet potato casserole topped with browned miniature marshmallows, green beans with slivered almonds, cranberry sauce, mashed potatoes, fruit salad, dinner rolls, and for dessert, apple, pumpkin, and minced meat pie topped with ice cream or whipped cream.

I still remember my grandfather's long prayer before we were allowed to eat. PaPa was a serious and grateful Christian man. I can still see myself barely cracking open one eyelid to see if my favorite cousin's eyes were closed during the prayer. When PaPa was praising God for our meal, I privately prayed to God to please encourage PaPa to get to his amen so we could eat.

After we celebrated with mother's family out on the farm, Daddy, Mother, my teenaged brother, and I joined my father's clan for Christmas dinner at their small home in town. The menu was almost the same as Christmas lunch on the farm, with one or two minor differences. I've carried those traditions into my own adult life. My daughter and I celebrate holidays in much the same way as I did when I was a child.

My mother was a great example of a hostess who loved cooking food for parties, neighbors, relatives, and for folks who needed a chef to help them celebrate a special occasion in our small town. She was a superb cook, as was Lynette, a dear friend of hers. Both were single—my mother widowed at age thirty-four in 1956 and Lynette unmarried—and both teachers in the local school district. Mother worked as the elementary school librarian in our hometown. Lynette was also a librarian at another school.

To make extra money on the side, Mother and Lynette started a business hosting parties for baby showers, birthdays, graduations, and rehearsal dinners for happy couples the evening before their wedding day. Some of the parties were large enough that Mother and Lynette hosted those sit-down dinners in Mother's backyard in Seminole. Seminole was a small West Texas town. Most everyone knew Mother and Lynette, so word of their catering business traveled fast.

Once I asked Mother, "Why do you and Lynette work so hard at this? You both have full-time jobs."

She grinned and said, "How else could two single women get invited to almost every important social gathering in town and get paid for it?"

That was Mother—she loved a party, but she was also resourceful. She grew up on a farm in Brownfield, Texas. Her dad—PaPa—was a dry land farmer, which meant there was no irrigation for the crops when Mother was a little girl. She'd learned how to make the best of everything. As a result, she knew how to stretch every dollar—a skill that served her well when Daddy died and she unexpectedly found herself a single mother of three children who had to work even harder to make ends meet.

Mother taught me how to make homemade candy—her favorites were divinity with a pecan half punched into the center of each piece, peanut patties, chocolate fudge with walnuts or pecans—and homemade angel food cake. Mother loved to make pumpkin bread and banana bread with pecans or walnuts for special friends during the Christmas holidays. She wrapped the loaves in holiday paper trimmed with ribbon. My favorite sweet treat Mother made was angel food cake with confetti sprinkles stirred into the batter. That cake always made it seem like we were having a party at home.

After Daddy died, Mother started making certain foods that she hadn't been able to prepare while he was alive, as they were too rich and not part of his heart-healthy diet. My favorite item that she introduced was Butter Horn Rolls, similar to Parker House Rolls. Not only did they taste delicious, but the aroma of the baking rolls wafting through the house evoked a sense of safety and loving warmth during a time when I desperately needed it.

Despite the comfort that my mother's cooking brought me, I learned early on that food does not always have to be shared to be enjoyable. The people who taught me this lesson were my mother's parents, Nennie and PaPa, with whom I spent a significant amount of time during summers on their farm in Brownfield, Texas.

PaPa's favorite summertime evening meal was an ice-cold glass of buttermilk with chunks of cornbread mixed in. He ate it with a long-handled spoon meant for stirring sugar in an iced tea glass. He appeared to relish it the same way I slurped up a thick vanilla malt.

Nennie didn't cook much because she had a busy interior design business. She was known throughout West Texas for her handmade draperies and upholstered furniture. During the week, I went to work with Nennie in town. By the time Nennie and I got home, PaPa would already have eaten, so the two of us would have our own supper together.

Over the years, I learned that Nennie and PaPa broke bread in different ways: sometimes separately, sometimes with each other, and with our entire extended family on certain holidays. They taught me that bowing one's head in silent prayer was fine too. As Nennie sometimes said, "We'll be grateful in our hearts," when I asked why we didn't pray in a restaurant.

Nennie and PaPa also helped me to realize that just because a person breaks bread alone sometimes doesn't mean a meal can't be just as memorable. I relish the solitary meals I intentionally plan. When I choose to eat at a favorite restaurant alone, I treat it as a special occasion. There are times that I get a strong craving for a special plate of enchiladas and guacamole with chips at a favorite Mexican restaurant or dream about the pasta dish I always order at an Italian restaurant in San Antonio. I catch myself savoring the meal in my mind's eye a day or two before I go. I purposely don't invite a friend to join me because it is my time to make a list of things I want to accomplish or to simply enjoy my own company. Without setting time aside for just me, I can get so busy I forget to be grateful. I frequently think of Nennie and PaPa and say a private prayer. I am thankful in my heart.

My paternal grandmother, Maw Maw, was a widow like my mother. Her husband died of a heart attack about a year after Daddy died. She worked in the cafeteria at the hospital in Brownfield. A taxi cab picked her up for work at 5:30 a.m. every weekday. She was not a person of means, but she was kind and grateful and the leader of the Decker clan. She lived in a tiny house that was warm with love and welcoming.

Maw Maw was a formidable canasta player. My brother and I visited on her days off and played canasta for hours at the kitchen table that almost filled her small kitchen. I chose a chair that faced the refrigerator. To my left was a floor-to-ceiling pantry covered by a cloth curtain and filled with canned foods and dried foods like macaroni noodles, pinto beans, black eyed peas, and navy beans.

While we were there, Maw Maw cooked for us. Even though she was a woman of few means, she invariably served everyone's favorite foods. As I got older, I marveled at her ability to begin with a can of store-bought vegetables and doctor them up so that they were delicious. A meal with Maw Maw was an event. It reminded me of the Thanksgiving *Saturday Evening Post* cover illustrating the "Freedom from Want" by Norman Rockwell from March 3, 1943. Maw Maw's careful and loving preparation of food for our entire family may not have appeared to be as fantastic as the meal depicted on the *Saturday Evening Post*, but to our family Maw Maw's table over-loaded with luscious dishes was spectacular and we understood her sacrifice to serve it.

The most memorable celebrations when I was a youngster revolved around sharing special meals with family and good friends. After Daddy died, Mother built the new house she and Daddy had planned to build on Fourteenth Street, four blocks over from Tenth Street where we lived when Daddy was alive. Our next-door neighbors were Eleanor and Thomas Plummer. The Plummers owned a ranch close to Levelland, about sixty miles from Seminole. I'll never forget when they invited our family to their cattle branding. They had been friends of my family for years and went to the First Baptist Church too.

As I got older and began to have trouble at school, Mrs. Plummer started inviting me over to their house for cooking lessons. The most important dish she taught me to make was egg custard pie. Learning to make a pie crust was tedious, and I had many failures before I was successful. Mrs. Plummer was patient but her standards were high. Many times, we threw my disasters in the trash and began again.

I didn't continue baking egg custard pie as I grew older, but Mrs. Plummer's interest and patience with me is a gift I've never forgotten. I seldom make an egg custard pie, but when I do, I am confident that Mrs. Plummer would be proud of the pie, with one exception. Instead of making my own pie crust, I buy it pre-made at the supermarket.

As I grew older, my taste buds evolved, as did my food favorites. One of my favorites was fried calf livers and onions, as well as fried chicken livers. They were also favorites of Mother's. When I married Larry and we were poor students at Texas Tech, he taught me to eat boiled chicken gizzards. It may sound awful to some, but once we added salt and pepper accompanied with ketchup, we were satisfied. In fact, boiled chicken gizzards became one of my favorites. A plus about enjoying boiled chicken gizzards was they were inexpensive and easy to prepare. In my mind's eye, I can still see and hear Larry thanking God for our food before we ate our meager meal of chicken gizzards or fried chicken livers, nourishing food we enjoyed and could afford.

After Larry left for Vietnam and I deployed to The Menninger Clinic, I found the bountiful food options in the cafeteria overwhelming. I had not overcome my bulimia early on in my treatment and the fantastic desserts frightened me. I was part of a group of patients accompanied to the dining room by a mental health aide. Every time I got to the end of the cafeteria line where the desserts were displayed, I panicked. *What should I choose and how can I eat just one?* I cried out silently. Eating in the cafeteria with a group of patients helped me get over gorging myself on sugary desserts and later vomiting. Over time, eating with the group in the cafeteria became comfortable for me. I went from praying to God to help me choose only one dessert to thanking God for the wonderful desserts and the ability to take just one and enjoy it.

Breaking bread with my fellow patients was a major part of my treatment. For too long during the time I was bulimic, I had perceived food as the enemy. As I began to heal, it started to feel like a gift from the universe.

Over the years and throughout my career, I've enjoyed preparing food for my students, colleagues, community officials, and board of education members. It's been a way to give back to the communities I've served and to say, "Thank you for your support."

My first teaching position was at East Topeka Junior High in Topeka, Kansas, the place where the famous *Brown v. Board of Education* case determined that children could no longer be segregated based on race. When I taught at East Topeka Junior High School, the student population was predominately Hispanic and African American.

During those years when I was teaching seventh, eighth, and ninth grade students, I asked them if they would like to bring food from home that represented their particular culture. The answer from the students and their parents was a resounding "Yes!" I asked my students and their parents to let me know the foods their family would offer so that I could personally add food that no one else was serving. The list of food that the children were bringing made it clear to me they'd grown up eating what I grew up eating, Mexican food and Southern food. As a result, I provided the condiments.

Later in the semester, I asked the lovely elderly Jewish lady who altered my clothes if she made matzo ball soup. "Of course," was her reply. Even though the school was interracial, I felt as if I had left out the opportunity for children to experience something they knew little of. Perhaps I still remembered my Jewish grade school friend Ellen from Seminole. One day toward the end of one of my seventh-grade classes, I passed a permission slip out to the students. I explained to parents that a good friend was preparing matzo ball soup for the children who would like to try it and that it was a Jewish staple. Most all of the children remembered to bring their permission slips, and I don't recall anyone saying no.

When I walked into class carrying two gallons of green liquid with huge bobbing matzo balls, I thought the children would never stop imitating gagging on it. Some who tried it thought it was delicious. Others turned up their noses. The point is, they learned about the food of another culture they had not encountered before and realized we are all more alike than different.

When I was superintendent of Stoughton public schools in the early eighties, there was a disconnect between some members of the community, the board, and the staff as the district had struggled with constructive salary negotiations in the past. To boost morale, I asked the cafeteria staff at the high school if they would help me prepare my chili recipe for lunch for the entire district staff on our upcoming institute day. I took my chili recipe and asked if it was doable. My recipe served 90 people, which would not have been enough, so the cafeteria staff more than doubled the recipe. They were gracious and kind. When I asked if I could help with the preparations and serve on the serving line, they seemed pleased that their work and importance to the school district was a major highlight that in-service day. When I explained to the board members that I had made arrangements to help make the chili for lunch for the district employees, they too wanted to serve meals to their employees. It felt like a turnaround for me. One could almost watch the tension between board members and district employees fade away.

Once everyone was served, board members, administrators, teachers, teacher aides, bus drivers, ground workers, and custodians all sat down to break bread. I heard conversations about one another's children, parents, and the students we served.

In 1993, the second year I served as superintendent of schools in River Forest, I desperately wanted to demonstrate my appreciation to the school staff, PTO members, and board of education members, so I decided to host a Brisket and Chili Day to honor them.

Because of the Texas menu and with the staff fully aware of my West Texas heritage, I decided to dress in my favorite Texas garb. At the time I was taking horseback riding lessons. I purchased a beautiful red suede riding jacket trimmed with light brown suede fringe the color of a bay horse. I wore that with a long black denim skirt that stopped at the lower part of my calf so that the beautiful stitching on the boot shaft of the handmade boots I wore was visible. Those boots had been made by an older cowboy I'd met in Fort Davis, Texas, who'd displayed a handwritten cardboard sign behind his chair that said, "Handmade Boots." I was skeptical but decided to take a chance to have a pair of handmade red cowboy boots. I wrote out a check for three hundred dollars and gave it to the gentleman, along with my home address in Illinois. In broken English, he explained that he worked in his small shop in Mexico and that I should expect my boots in five to six weeks. We shook hands and I left wondering if I'd ever see my boots.

Six weeks later, when I arrived home from work, the postman had delivered a package. I tore into the carefully wrapped package and was thrilled. My red boots were gorgeous and fit perfectly. I wore them every Brisket and Chili Day after that.

My red boots symbolized a personal event, and the community and staff appreciated me being who I was and sharing my background with them. Together we created a gestalt, a tradition of sharing food together partnered with a new tradition. Every year we ate together, shared stories, and recognized our differences and our similarities.

Nothing satisfied me more than watching someone enjoying my barbecue brisket and Texas chili made and served by my own hands. I ladled chili into bowl after bowl and offered sprinkles of green onion and grated cheese, topped off with a bit of Tabasco sauce to add a special blast of flavor. One member of our board of education insisted on baking Mexican cornbread to accompany it.

I always had the brisket party before the winter break to celebrate the upcoming holiday season. I loved cooking for the community and saying, "Thank you and happy holidays," as I personally served each guest. During all those years when I was cooking for my colleagues, I learned more food is better than less since I was horrified of the prospect of running out of food. One time I ordered thirteen briskets from a local meat market. Each brisket weighed between ten to twelve pounds. I planned three servings per pound. I began cooking on Friday night and finished during the early morning hours on Monday. I set the alarm during the night so I could get up when they were ready to slice, add the barbeque sauce, rewrap each brisket with new aluminum foil, and cook them for one more hour. I cooked large vats of chili on the stove top at the same time.

We estimated we served between 200 and 250 guests. The invitation list included elected board presidents and the executive administrators representing the River Forest Public Library, the River Forest Village Board, the River Forest Park District, the River Forest Township, Thrive Counseling Center, and the neighboring Oak Park Elementary School District and Oak Park/River Forest High School. Private schools included Grace Lutheran School, St. Luke Parish School, and Keystone Montessori. The presidents of Dominican University and Concordia University also joined us along with guests they invited from their universities.

Mother even got into the act and mailed her homemade peanut patties and pecan brittle, both authentic Texas treats. I admit, I ordered boxes of cookies from the bakery as well to ensure everyone had the opportunity to satisfy their sweet tooth.

The condiments were typical: corn chips and dip, crackers, pickled jalapeño peppers, fresh baked rolls for the brisket if guests preferred a brisket sandwich, and pinto beans.

The brisket party was a marvelous way to give back and offer gratitude to hardworking teachers, staff, and community members who volunteered their time to lead our school district. I was exhausted at the end of the day, but I never questioned whether the work and the time was worth it.

# YOUR TURN

·····················

Breaking bread with family, friends, and even strangers gives us the opportunity to share stories and to get to know someone we've considered a casual acquaintance, and often signals to us that we have more in common with others than we might have thought. Eating with someone often leads to a discussion of the foods we like and don't like. For example, if I say, "This food on the buffet is too salty for me. What do you think?" the other person may respond with, "My doctor says Americans eat too much salt, but I grew up dousing my food with salt," or, "As a teenager, I loved fresh hot French fries covered with salt, which made me thirsty so I chased the fries down with huge swigs of Coca-Cola," or, "Since I've been diagnosed with high blood pressure, I've had to pull back on the salt."

All of a sudden, your eating partner has just shared something very personal with you. From there, the conversation flows more naturally and can go almost anywhere. It's almost as if eating food together or breaking bread across the table from someone demands conversation at the table. For me, nothing is more uncomfortable than sitting at a table with someone I don't know and eating silently rather than having a friendly conversation. If the other party doesn't want to talk, I've learned to keep my mouth shut, though that's not natural for me. It's also valuable to eat alone sometimes, taking time just to be quiet and enjoy the scenery, to reflect on your day, to relish certain foods, or to read a good book while you eat.

Think back to some of your most memorable meals. Write about the good times—and the bad, if you wish—that those experiences generated. Share stories about your fellow diners, the holidays you spent with them, the specific foods you shared, and any special recipes that you love to prepare.

**What was it like at the beginning of the story?** Include the facts—where you were, when the event took place, who was there, and how you felt.

**What happened?** Write the story like you would tell it verbally. Use active language and give examples. Include as much detail as possible to vividly recreate the scene. Most important, what was the issue? Was there a problem, a tragedy, a celebration?

**What was it like at the end of the story?** For me, the most important stories are those that teach us something. What did you learn from your experience? In writing *Where the Water Meets the Sand*, I realized that many of the lessons I learned in childhood, I later utilized and appreciated as an adult.

## TYRA'S BARBECUE BRISKET

**YIELD:** Plan for three servings per pound. (An 8–12-pound brisket is 24–36 servings.)

**Ingredients**
1  8–12 lb. brisket
Salt
Black pepper

**Directions**
Preheat oven to 250°F.

Rub approximately 1½ teaspoons salt and 1 teaspoon pepper into brisket (vary the amount of seasoning based on the size of your brisket).

Wrap brisket in heavy aluminum foil so that air can't escape (2 sheets are best). Place brisket in roasting pan.

Place brisket in 250-degree oven for five to six hours depending on the size. Take brisket out, unwrap, and cool. Throw out the grease.

Slice the brisket in thin to medium slices.

Place the slices of brisket in 2 new heavy aluminum foil sheets.

Before wrapping, pour one whole bottle of barbeque sauce over it. (I prefer Master-piece Barbeque Sauce.)

Be sure the sauce flows down between the slices. Depending on the size of the brisket, you may need more than one bottle of sauce.

Heat brisket one more hour at 250 degrees.

If you choose not to use barbeque sauce because it is too messy and you want to serve brisket for sandwiches, omit the salt and pepper, add one package of Lipton Onion Soup Mix sprinkled on top of the brisket, and follow the remaining directions.

## TYRA'S CHILI

**YIELD:** 90 servings (You can reduce the amount of chili by dividing the ingredients by 10 for 9 servings, and so on.)

**Ingredients**
13½ lbs of lean hamburger
4½ tall cans tomato juice
2½ gallons of pinto or ranch beans
6 pkg instant chili mix
10 medium onions
18 tablespoons salt

## Directions

Brown hamburger meat and onions together. I prefer using a large cast-iron skillet. Add instant chili mix and simmer. (The amount of water you use will be on the back of your instant chili mix package)

Combine beans, water, salt, and tomato juice in a kettle. When the mixture is hot, add the hamburger, onions, and instant chili mix. Cook 1½ hours, stirring occasionally. Add more salt and chili mix to taste. Also add water if the chili gets too thick, but don't add too much. The goal is to create a thick chili.

# CHAPTER 13:

# Families We Choose,

# Families Who Choose Us

My mother was not only my most significant family member but also the person who taught me to love my neighbor. She modeled the importance of making good friends. From as early as I can remember, my family lived close to both all of our relatives and our dear friends. These people, some of whom knew me when I was as young as two years old until they passed away from old age or illness in their later years, will forever live in my heart.

Ida Mae and P.D. who lived next door were like family. We celebrated Christmas with them every year and we celebrated our birthdays together. When one of us faced trials, illnesses, or deaths in our families, we were always there for each other. As a youngster, I considered them like family and I placed them on a pedestal. They had no children and didn't have to put up with us, but they loved us and we knew it.

One of mother's best friends also lived close by, down the street from our house in the next block. She and her husband owned a restaurant in town and she went to our church. Almost any time we went to town, we'd stop by the restaurant to have a cup of coffee and a Coke before going home. Their two boys and my brother and I played kick the can during the summer months. When the oldest son died of a brain tumor not long after he started his work as a minister, it felt as if one of our own had died. Not a friend, but a member of our family.

I lived on Tenth Street. My best friend lived a block over on Ninth. Our birthdays were only three days apart. As a result, we almost always were in the same class, from first grade through junior high school. I hung out at her house and she played at mine. Her mother and my mother were close too. As we grew older, we weren't as close, but I will never forget the sense of being home whenever I went to her house. I have strong, comforting memories of her family visiting mine the day my father died when I was nine. My friend's parents and my mother stayed close until they couldn't.

As I grew older and after my father died, for the first time in my life, Mother went to work. She got a job as a PBX telephone operator at Seminole Public Schools in our hometown. She also completed as many college correspondence courses at Texas Tech as she was allowed. At that point, we moved to Alpine, a small town close to Big Bend National Park, so that Mother could finish her bachelor's degree and become an elementary school teacher.

That year was like heaven for me. Alpine was nestled in the mountains, so different from Seminole and the expansive nothingness of the plains of West Texas. At night the skies in Alpine were coal black and the night stars sparkled like diamonds on a black velvet evening dress. The most important and memorable lovely thing was that I made brand-new friends. Some lived on ranches, some lived in town, some of their parents worked at the university, and others stayed home or had businesses in town. Having spent my life in Seminole, I felt as if I had a new life, a new family, a new tribe.

## FAMILY BY CIRCUMSTANCE

There are times in almost everyone's life when we establish close relationships with individuals because of circumstances. At first, many of us feel vulnerable when we make major moves, like leaving home and moving into a dorm our first year at the university, but we often develop close relationships with roommates and become friends with our classmates and others we meet through the friendships we've formed. We carry memories of these special relationships with us throughout our lives, although we don't physically see these friends or continue to stay in touch with them once we move on. In my case, a small number of friends have remained close although my interaction with them is sporadic. I've already shared stories of the many colleagues who became like family to me during my long career as an educator in the "Breaking Bread" chapter. I will never forget those allies who supported me in our shared professional communities. The following are stories of other characters outside my work world who became as close to me as my own kin.

## OLLIE

When I was a pregnant teenager, I lived in Abilene, Texas, with an older woman who kept "girls like me" until my baby was born. Her name was Ollie and the program was sponsored by the Church of Christ in Abilene Texas. Ollie became like family to me. My grandmother Nennie came to visit me several times on weekends and stayed overnight at Ollie's house with me. The three of us ate meals together and told stories as if we were family. Nennie and Ollie became good friends. Both Ollie and I looked forward to her visits.

Ollie invited me to watch television with her when she came home for lunch during the work week. We'd take our lunch into her large bedroom suite and living area and watch *As the World Turns*.

"You're not like the other girls who've stayed here until their babies were born," she told me one day. "You're different, like family," she said as she hugged me close.

"How am I different?" I asked.

I'll never forget her response. "You treat me like family. Not like a landlord," she said.

Even as a teenager who depended on the help and support of strangers, I realized that so many of us at one time or another are lonely and long for the warmth of friendship and love.

Ollie will live in my heart forever. Every time I hear the words, "the kindness of strangers," I think of her. She saved my life, loved me, and took me in.

After Larry and I married and Laura was born, Larry's father, the chief master sergeant, was stationed at Dyess Air Force Base outside of Abilene, Texas, where I'd lived with Ollie. I asked Larry if he would go with me and meet Ollie. I wanted to introduce her to our baby, Laura. Larry had heard all the details of my teenage pregnancy and often spoke of his gratitude for Ollie and the Church of Christ who supported me and took care of me until my baby was born.

Larry's response was a resounding yes. Ollie was thrilled to hear from me and excited to meet Larry and Laura. I'll never forget how I felt when Larry pulled the car up to the curb at Ollie's. A wave of fear and dread washed over me. Giving up my baby girl was something I tried not to dwell on, something I kept in a safe secret space in my heart. I only shared it with those whom I trusted completely.

As we walked up to Ollie's door, I started to walk faster as Larry carried Laura. I barely had time to knock twice when Ollie opened the door. She looked just as I remembered her, perhaps a bit shorter. Her hair had more gray in it, but her angelic smile was the same. She reached for Larry's hand, squeezed it, and wrapped her arms around my waist. As soon as we sat down, she reached for Laura as she simultaneously asked, "May I hold her?" A part of me felt as if I had come home, home to a place where I had been safe, loved, and protected. I whispered a prayer of thanksgiving that Larry, Ollie, and Laura were all together with me. I watched as Ollie oohed and aahed over Laura. Larry grinned from ear to ear. He was comfortable with Ollie.

"This is a great place you have," he said. "Thank you for caring for Tyra when she didn't have anyone to help her out."

*How could it be better than this*, I thought. *No need for secrets. No lies. No embarrassment and no judgment. Thank you, God. I am so grateful.*

## THE MENNINGER FAMILY

After Larry was deployed to Vietnam, I fell apart and deployed to The Menninger Clinic. Once I was escorted to the tiny room that would become my home for eight months, my inner voice screamed, *What have you done, you idiot? You must be crazy to hospitalize yourself in this locked-down place. You earned this for the crazy things you do.* Exhausted, I fell asleep on the twin bed pushed against the wall.

Over time, though, I learned to trust my house doctor and became close friends with some of the patients. Eventually, I looked forward to leaving the ward with the group to go down to the dining room. Even though some of my patient friends were tongue thrusters and some stirred the food on their plate into unappetizing gobs, I began to appreciate them as family. We ate together in the dining room. I played chess almost every day with a patient who was a minister. These people were unpretentious and often unusual, but so was I. My own idiosyncrasies didn't seem so out of line anymore.

The day Dr. Roberts, my house doctor, told me that Larry had been killed in the Vietnam War, the staff told the other patients on the ward. I stayed in my room most of the day into the evening. I turned down dinner. Later that evening, a patient who "lived in a spaceship" knocked on my door and invited me to join her on her spaceship. I understood that she was offering to take me away to a place where I could avoid my pain. I said, "No, Emily, your spaceship's not real." Emily immediately turned and shuffled down the hall in her Scandinavian clogs.

Not long after, another patient knocked on the door and invited me to join the group in the patient lounge. "I'm so sorry, come be with us. Don't be alone," she cajoled. "I have a new record album by James Taylor, *Sweet Baby James.*" I did join the group in the lounge. They were all there; even the most ill among us understood that my husband had been killed and reached out to give their condolences in their own way. I will never forget the kindness and love given to me that night. Penny met me at the door of the lounge and led me to a seat of honor. George brought me a cup of instant coffee from the snack bar. Cassandra sat on the floor across the room, rocking her body back and forth as she often did and chanting, "Jesus in my mind's eye, Jesus in my mind's eye," as if she was praying for Jesus's intervention. Skylar sat on the floor near Cassandra, her painted cherry-red lips plunging downward into a frown, a testament to her ability to comprehend the sadness of the occasion.

When people find out I had been hospitalized at Menninger, the famous mental health hospital, some say, "Oh Tyra, you weren't like those people."

My response always is, "You have to understand, I had the credentials. Some of the patients were my dear friends. I loved them. They were part of my family."

## MOTHERHOOD

Larry and I were so excited when we learned I was pregnant. I had preeclampsia again just as I had with my first pregnancy, but Laura was born perfectly formed, with ten toes and ten fingers. At the time of her birth, Larry, who was attending flight school to earn his pilot's wings, was up in the air. I was told Larry called me immediately after landing his plane, leaving the flight line and washing up.

We had decided ahead of time that if our baby was a girl we'd name her Laura Elizabeth after Larry and my younger sister, Beth. As soon as Laura and I were discharged from the hospital, my mother, grandmother Nennie, my younger sister, and some of my dad's relatives came to see Laura. We lived in a small duplex close to Reese Air Force Base in Lubbock. I had dropped out of school the semester our baby was due. Almost six months after Laura was born, we were able to move into base housing at Reese, close to the flight line and the commissary. After taking a semester off, I returned to school, and a family friend kept Laura during the day while I attended college classes.

After Larry was killed, the air force moved our trailer house from Lubbock, Texas, to Topeka, Kansas, where Laura and I started our new lives as a family of two. Even though I was finishing my bachelor's degree, I always made sure we had quality time together.

We went to the park, waded at the edge of Lake Shawnee, and went out to eat together, but our favorite activity was baking sugar cookies. Even though Laura was barely three years old, she helped decorate the freshly baked cookies for Halloween, her favorite holiday. I wrapped an apron around her, gave her a big plastic bowl of icing, and let her do it herself. She loved to spread tons of frosting all over the cookies, and then she'd cover the cookies with bright yellow-and-orange candy corn. I loved watching her do it.

"Look, Mommy," she'd squeal each time she added one more piece of candy corn to each cookie.

"Beautiful," I'd encourage her, grateful I had wrapped the entire tabletop with Saran wrap. Afterward, I stripped her down to her birthday suit and dipped her into a warm tub of bath water and baby bubble bath soap.

I spent as much time as I could with Laura and studied for my classes after I put her to bed. Our lives were full and rich, though I missed Larry terribly. After studying, I'd listen to the tapes of recorded music on the stereo set that had been sent back to me after Larry was killed.

After I finished my bachelor's degree, I dated a man who loved Laura and with whom Laura was infatuated. I hated the thought of Laura growing up without a father, and he and I married. Laura and Kenneth had a great relationship, yet over time, I realized I wasn't over Larry Hull and asked Kenneth for a divorce. The two of us agreed to tell Laura together. We decided to tell her on a Saturday so we'd have the weekend to discuss any follow-up questions she might have.

When we told her we were going to divorce, I took the lead and said, "Laura, I have asked Kenneth for a divorce."

Laura stamped her foot. "Mom, why?" she asked, as she crawled into Kenneth's lap and cried. I felt like a witch, but I knew I was doing the right thing. Kenneth stayed close to Laura and I was grateful.

Ten years after Larry's death, I confronted my addiction to alcohol and joined a support group for people who were trying to quit drinking. I sat down with Laura and explained, "I want to tell you that I have a drinking problem. I've tried to stop drinking on my own, but I haven't been able to stop."

"Really, Mom?" Laura quipped. "I live with you. Did you think I didn't know?"

I hugged her and told her I had made a decision to quit drinking. Laura agreed to go to an open meeting for people who had decided to quit drinking and their families who were supportive of them. We attended the group meeting every Saturday night while we still lived in Kansas. We both enjoyed the camaraderie, especially when we went out for coffee and desserts after the meeting.

About the same time, Laura landed the star role in the annual school play at her middle school as the town's heroine, Willie Lovelace, in *Blazing Guns at Roaring Gulch*. Friends from the support group attended the play to show their support. Laura stayed active in the teens' group for those whose parents were alcoholic, and I also stayed active in the support group until we moved to Highland Park, Illinois, when I accepted a new position as the director for instruction.

When Laura enrolled at Highland Park High School as a sophomore, I was acutely aware of the sacrifice she was making, since she'd started school in Topeka and had left her best friends and confidants to enroll in a new high school in another town and state.

Fortunately, within ten days of attending school, she announced she'd met a group of girls at the school who had reached out to her. A few days later, she was late getting home from school, even though the walk was only three blocks. Even though she was a high schooler, I felt edgy she wasn't home when I got home from work. About the time my edginess started to turn into worry, she bounded in the front door, grinning from ear to ear.

"Mom, some friends of mine and I are trying out for the play!"

I exhaled deeply and didn't bother to mention my previous worry. I said simply, "Oh Laura, I'm thrilled!"

Our dinner conversation was different that night. Rather than me struggling to get Laura to tell me about her school day, she chattered on and on about the play and the friends she had met. Highland Park was a wonderful community of people who showed their support for education through their involvement in the schools and the funds they contributed to ensure the best possible education for their children.

Laura was hired by a law firm as a part-time clerical staff member in Highland Park after school when she was a high school junior and senior. She adored the people in the law office and worked hard. One morning before leaving for school, she reminded me she had an appointment to get her hair styled after work. Laura was a senior and excited to be attending the prom. I'll never forget when she came home from the beauty shop with a punk haircut. My reaction was to remind Laura that prom was coming up and blah blah blah—until I remembered some of the decisions I had made as a teenager. Although initially I was appalled, I couldn't help but remember some of the off-the-charts things I'd done as a teenager and kept my real opinions to myself. "Well," I said. "That's the style these days. Right?"

Laura wore a beautiful dress for senior prom, and I made sure when I took photographs of her that the side of her hair in the photo was the side with longer hair rather than the shaved side. To this day, I wish I'd taken photos of both sides of her amazing hairstyle.

After Laura went to college on the East Coast, I found myself out of sorts. She and I were close and the house felt empty like a cave. After six years in Highland Park,

I applied for my first superintendent position and moved to Stoughton, Wisconsin, just fifteen miles south of Madison. I enjoyed my work in Stoughton and spent most weekends in Madison, shopping and meeting friends for lunch. Stoughton was barely one hundred miles north of Highland Park, so I'd return to Chicago to indulge in the Chicago Lyric Opera. However, I gave up the Chicago Symphony. I didn't want to be a fly-by-night superintendent and went to as many school events as I could in Stoughton.

Laura graduated from college with a degree in hospitality and moved to Madison. She lived with me for a while in Stoughton until she found an apartment. She began a second degree in computer information systems and graduated.

---

I moved back to the Chicago area two years later when I was invited to apply for the superintendent position in River Forest, Illinois. I felt terrible leaving the school district in Stoughton after just two years, but I was thrilled to be back in Chicagoland. Laura stayed in Madison. We took turns visiting one another on weekends every four to six weeks.

I thoroughly enjoyed my time in River Forest District 90 and stepped down to retire from the superintendent position after serving the district for twelve years. It was the summer of 2004. In August of the same year, Laura purchased an amazing surprise birthday gift for my fifty-seventh birthday. She purchased tickets for the two of us to attend a concert starring two of my very favorite artists, Willie Nelson and Bob Dylan, at Warner Field, the minor league ballpark, in Madison, Wisconsin.

When she told me the news, I beamed and said, "Oh, Laura, I've never seen either one in person! This is the best possible gift you could have given me."

The night of the concert, we sat on the grass up close to the stage. I will never forget that opportunity to spend time with my daughter and two of my favorite entertainers performing at the same venue. After taking a seven-month break from work, I went to work at Dominican University in River Forest. I enjoyed my work there, especially getting to know the nuns and the students. But I was anxious to move back to Texas to be closer to my mother, who was becoming more and more fragile as she aged.

In 2008, I moved home to Texas to serve as director of education at Sul Ross in Alpine, Texas, where my mother had earned her bachelor's degree. Laura decided to work remotely for the technology information company she worked for in Chicago and moved to Texas so she could be closer to me after I was diagnosed with cancer. She loves Texas as I do. We always see each other on holidays and visit one another when we can. All these years, we have made a point of staying close. Our family may be small, but it is strong.

# YOUR TURN

..................................................

Think about the people closest to you. Are they blood relatives whom you love and would choose to spend quality time with even if they weren't your relatives? And do you have other blood relatives whom you care about because you're related but with whom you have little in common? Does that make them seem less like family to you?

What about the people you love and respect and want to spend as much time as possible with even though they are not your blood relatives? Do you consider them to be more like family than some in your family of origin?

Think about some of your most memorable times with any of the people who comprise your version of family, and write those stories. Describe what you learned from your times with them, and celebrate the people you've adopted or who have adopted you.

**What was it like at the beginning of the story?** Include the facts—where you were, when the event took place, who was there, and how you felt.

**What happened?** Write the story like you would tell it verbally. Use active language and give examples. Include as much detail as possible to vividly recreate the scene. Most important, what was the issue? Was there a problem, a tragedy, a celebration?

**What was it like at the end of the story?** For me, the most important stories are those that teach us something. What did you learn from your experience? In writing *Where the Water Meets the Sand*, I realized that many of the lessons I learned in childhood, I later utilized and appreciated as an adult.

# CHAPTER 14:

# The Gift of Music

..................................................

Music has the power to change the world, to change people, and to change a bad day into a more hopeful one. In several previous chapters, I have written about particular songs and how they gave me hope or brought me together with others. That is why it feels appropriate for music to be the focus for my last chapter.

I listen to music for inspiration when I write, when I feel ungrateful or grateful, or when I feel lonely—or when I don't. I listen to music whenever I can. My musical taste is eclectic, ranging from classical music to a deep and abiding love for the country music I grew up with, but what all my favorite songs have in common is that they make my soul soar and remind me that my spirit is strong.

I grew up attending the Southern Baptist Church in my hometown. When I was a child, my favorite part of the service was the music. Then Daddy brought an old player piano home for me. I took lessons and I was hooked as a child. Over time, I learned to play classical music revised for beginners until I improved over almost ten years of lessons to the real thing. I have a deep appreciation for classical music and try to do it justice when I play pieces by Bach, Mozart, Wagner, and Brahms. I played "Für Elise" by Beethoven for my last recital.

Most of the time when I took piano lessons, I played in group recitals where other students also performed. Our school district offered band in sixth grade. I chose the flute as my instrument since flute music and piano music were very similar. When we moved to Alpine so Mother could finish her bachelor's degree, I continued to play the flute as a seventh grader and took piano lessons. My piano teacher in Alpine was adamant that I have an individual recital, just me playing my repertoire. My last recital was in Brownfield, forty miles from my hometown where my grandmother lived and where I took lessons. It was my last year of taking piano lessons. I was a sophomore in high school.

It would be eleven years before I was able to purchase a piano. In the meantime, I satisfied my urge for music by listening to the radio and record albums. Larry purchased an amazing stereo, amplifier, two huge speakers, and headphones while he was in Vietnam. After he died, I'd listen to the reel-to-reel double-sided tapes Larry had recorded from his colleagues in Vietnam. Years later, I had the tapes recorded on CDs so I'll always have Larry's music.

I bought a piano and began playing again after my second husband, Kenneth, and I divorced. Even though I often felt lonely, playing the piano lifted my spirits. I played popular music I purchased at music stores. I scrounged through cardboard boxes in storage until I found my old Baptist hymnal and played my old favorites, singing at the top of my lungs. It took me back to my childhood, when family was close and I felt less alone.

During the River Forest Memorial Day Parade, I played my flute with the Roosevelt Middle School band on their float. I loved joining the students and the community during parades and celebrations. It's difficult to find ways to interact with students once you become superintendent of a school district. Participating in student activities communicated that I knew who the most important people in the district were—the students. They always welcomed me and seemed excited I wanted to join them, and they ignored my mistakes if I missed a note.

Music has the power to transform an average day into something magical. If you're lucky enough to experience it in a live performance, it's even more special. Fortunately, I've lived close to live performance venues throughout most of my life.

I took advantage of the concerts in Kansas City when I lived in Topeka. Patti LaBelle and the Blue Belles and Gladys Knight and the Pips were at the top of my favorite music list in the mid-seventies, partially because they helped me connect with the music so many of my African American and Hispanic students were listening to during my first teaching job at East Topeka Junior High School. I was thrilled on two occasions when I had the opportunity to attend their concerts. I went to both concerts with an African American friend from the school where I taught. She and I taught a team-teaching class. As we entered the auditorium, I realized I was one of the few white people in the audience. I didn't care. I was with my friend and felt comfortable.

When Patti and the Blue Belles danced out on the stage singing, it felt as if the entire auditorium, including the building, the seats, stage, and most of all the audience and performers, swayed and rocked with the beat of the music as one. When the audience started to sing along, I did too. I felt as though I belonged, and I was surprised that I felt so uninhibited. Everyone was there to hear the music. The notes, rhythm, and voices surrounded us as we all sang along. For that time, we were one. To this day, whenever I listen to Motown music, I feel the Motown beat reverberate down my spine. If I'm in my car alone, I sing at the top of my lungs. I remember the good times, the children I taught during my time at East Topeka, the friends I knew and still communicate with, and I remember the music I was introduced to during the critical times in my life. Most of all, the music reminds me of a time when people of a different race welcomed me, embraced me, reached out to me, cared about me, and included me.

I wanted to see Gladys Knight and the Pips when they performed in Kansas City and I invited my friend again. She was all in. This time I felt more comfortable since

I had attended Patti LaBelle's concert. The concert was in the same venue and the audience was similar. This time, I felt right at home. The song "Midnight Train to Georgia" was one of my favorites. This time, when the crowd jumped to their feet, I joined them immediately and began to sway and dance in place. It was another wonderful concert where I felt I belonged. The color of my skin or that of the other members of the audience didn't matter. The music brought us together. That's what music does. It brings us together in song and sometimes embrace. What could be better than that?

During the 1980s, I fell in love with the Ravinia Festival when Laura and I lived in Highland Park, Illinois. Almost immediately after I began my position at Highland Park School District 108, the superintendent invited Laura and me to join his family for the first of what became many concerts I enjoyed there.

First opened in 1904, Ravinia Festival is the oldest outdoor music festival in the United States and summer residency of the Chicago Symphony Orchestra. The thirty-six-acre park is situated north of Chicago in a beautiful wooded area. My friends and I always enjoyed listening to the music while having a picnic on the lawn. Whether the concerts were classical, jazz, pop, or country, they were all performed by first-class international performers.

My favorite Ravinia memory will always be the much-anticipated annual performance each July of Tchaikovsky's iconic "1812 Overture." I especially loved the growing anticipation among the audience as the performance got closer to its stunning final crescendo. For one moment, sitting there under the stars, thousands of us were transfixed—transported by the magic of musical genius and virtuosity back over two hundred years to a battlefield surrounded by the sound of cannons exploding everywhere. It was thrilling every single year. No other live musical performance has impacted me nor stayed with me like the "1812 Overture" at Ravinia. Each year, stretched out on my blanket staring upward at the black sky lit with the twinkling stars of heaven, I was sure there was no place I'd rather be.

Another high point of live music in Illinois was the Lyric Opera in downtown Chicago. Located in the heart of the city, the building is magnificent and is described as a hybrid of art nouveau and art deco styles. My seats always had a direct and clear view of the stage, and the sound was as if the vocalists were singing to me no matter where I sat. As I walked into the lobby the first time, I felt a sense of opulence wash over me. I could not recall ever being in a more exquisite concert hall.

Several operas stand out in my memory. *Salome*, which I saw performed by Maria Ewing in 1988, is one of my favorites, although it is described as depraved and the characters immoral. It drew such an emotional reaction from me and the rest of the audience, who were most often contained until the correct time to applaud or react. In addition, I had never seen a play nor an opera portraying the death of John the Baptist and the physical horror of it. When John's head was brought out on a platter, a curdling scream erupted from an audience member approximately six rows from where I sat. Because of the acoustics in the auditorium, everyone, including those in the balcony, heard it. I personally was relieved that someone communicated the horror of it all but grateful that I hadn't been the one to scream.

Another opera that changed me was *Madame Butterfly*. It was about a geisha girl, Ciocio-san, who ignored her family, her honor, and her fortune for an American naval officer named Pinkerton who dishonestly led the geisha to believe they would be married since he called her his bride. She gives birth to a baby son, though Pinkerton has deserted and misled her. She names the son Trouble. Given my experience as a teenaged unwed mother, my heart sank for her. And when the national tour of *Miss Saigon*, the successful musical based on the story of *Madame Butterfly*, opened in Chicago in 1992, this rendition of the Broadway musical was more personal for me since it was based on the Vietnam War which had left an indelible scar on Laura and me. Still, I loved it.

After retiring in 2004 from the River Forest School District, I felt empty and out of place. I decided after six months to go to work as the director of the Master's of Arts in Teaching Program at Dominican University. We were beyond thrilled when the board brought Renée Fleming to perform to raise money. She had been a favorite of mine since my experience at the Lyric and I was mesmerized. She sang some classical songs, some arias, and some pop tunes.

When Renée was interviewed about Senator John McCain's request that she sing "Danny Boy" at his funeral in 2018, she talked about the importance of music. She commented that listening to powerful music is a bonding experience that brings people together. Songs like "Danny Boy," "Amazing Grace," and "Ave Maria" mean something to us all. She went on to say, "Music is a language we relate to even as infants."

Music can also be a salve to the soul, especially when we're alone. At times, when I am driving out to West Texas from the Hill Country where I live, I can't wait to get on the road so I can drive for five to six hours, alone in my car. I am no vocalist and sing only when I am alone driving down the highway with the radio blaring. Then I sing my heart out, like I'm free as a bird. Driving down miles of highway, especially when I'm on the way to Alpine and I first see the pale outlines of the mountains, I start to hear "Somewhere Over the Rainbow" in my mind. It was a piece of music I played on the piano as a beginner. Once I admitted to a friend that whenever I first see the mountains of Big Bend from the highway, I think of "Somewhere Over the Rainbow" because it looks like the mountaintops are outlined in sparkling red and green magic markers. She stared at me as though I was making up the story, so I dropped it. Still, each time I take that road back to Alpine and the mountains, when the mountains come into view and I am alone, I often pull my car over to the edge of the highway and take out Eva Cassidy's rendition of "Somewhere Over the Rainbow" on CD from the storage box between my front seats.

As I pull back onto the highway, as always, it appears the mountaintops are lined with red and green sparkling magic markers. Are they, I wonder, or am I imagining it?

# YOUR TURN

.....................................

Think of the most important songs in your life. Why are they important? Do they remind you of people you will love forever even though they have passed away or moved on? Are those songs a tangible reminder, stamped on your psyche, of relationships, events, or eras?

Think of a love song you and your first significant other chose as "your song." Even though that young love may not have survived, when you hear that one special melody, you inevitably remember that boy or girl you loved, no matter how old you get.

That's what music does—it takes us back to a person, place, or time that we store in files in our brain so we can pull them out to relish a great love or to remember a hard lesson we learned.

Think back on some of your most memorable music experiences. Write about the good times—and the bad, if you wish. Share stories about the music you loved as a child, a teenager, and an adult, and describe how music represents aspects of your spirituality, personality, and psyche. What about a song that reminds you of a trip you took, like "El Condor Pasa" reminds me of Peru? Or a holiday song that turns your stomach or makes you laugh, like "Grandma Got Run Over by a Reindeer"? Try to describe your favorite and not-so-favorite memories and the soundtracks that impacted them.

**What is one of the most memorable musical experiences you've ever had?** Include the facts—where you were, when the event took place, who was there, and how you felt.

**What happened?** Write the story like you would tell it verbally. Use active language and give examples. Include as much detail as possible to vividly recreate the scene. Most important, what was the issue? Was there a problem, a tragedy, a celebration?

**What was it like at the end of the story?** For me, the most important stories are those that teach us something. What did you learn from your experience? In writing *Where the Water Meets the Sand*, I realized that many of the lessons I learned in childhood, I later utilized and appreciated as an adult.

This is the last chapter. Now, it really is your turn. Enjoy!

# Acknowledgments

...................................................

The author gratefully acknowledges Brooke Warner and her entire publishing team at She Writes Press. Their patience and hard work to ensure that *Your Turn: Ways to Celebrate Life Through Storytelling* would be concise and focused on my goals to encourage readers to tell and write their own stories was phenomenal. I particularly enjoyed working with Lauren Wise. She is knowledgeable and was determined from the start to ensure that *Your Turn* would be well written. I will always appreciate her focus on creating the best possible finished book. Annie Tucker is an amazing editor, thorough and accurate. I appreciate her encouragement, her skill, and consistency. The members of Brooke's professional team are hard-working advocates for writers and were consistently available promptly when I had questions.

Crystal Patriarche's team at SparkPoint Studio is amazing. They have provided marketing opportunities resulting in recognition for *Your Turn* in numerous media publications including *Parade Magazine*, PsychCentral and *Kirkus Reviews*. They have also managed ongoing chances to place *Your Turn* before those who love stories and appreciate the love of writing. Special appreciation to Tabitha Bailey and Madison Ostrander at SparkPoint.

I'd also like to acknowledge Gardi and Brad Wilks of Wilks Communications Group, who manage my website (tyramanning.com), and review and post my weekly blogs. They are also irreplaceable helpers when organizing speaking opportunities in Chicagoland.

Marianne Turney tirelessly reviewed my first rough drafts. Additionally, I am thrilled and immensely grateful for the reviews written by amazing and thoughtful readers. I met Bridget Boland in 2004 at a seminar for writers at the Ragdale Foundation in Lake Forest, Illinois north of Chicago. Bridget Boland has been on my team since 2006. She is a friend and amazing writing coach.

An extra-special shout-out goes to Nolan Brohaugh, my social worker when I was a patient at The Menninger Clinic from 1970 to 1971, who has become a dear friend over the years.

Last and not least, I thank Dr. Walt Menninger of the famous Menninger Clinic. He and his family have become friends since his precious wife, Connie, was my PTO President after I left the Clinic and was hired at Boswell Junior High and Robinson Middle School in Topeka, Kansas.

Thank you all.

# About the Author

As a former educator, I will always associate fall with the start of the school year—bells ringing in the hallways, sharpening of brand-new pencils, cracking the spine of a textbook for the first time. While I've been retired from the profession for some time, I haven't left the academic world behind entirely.

Like my former students, I have had my own writing deadlines to meet, which has meant many late nights in front of the computer, rounds of edits, and cheerful celebrations when I submit another chapter.

I've always believed that creative expression, through writing, helps us uncover gems of hope and serenity and navigate difficult times. Sharing stories with one another fills the space between us, inspires us, helps us forge stronger relationships, and teaches us that we're more alike than different.

In *Your Turn* I offer examples of stories from my own life and give readers an invitation to delve into their own emotional histories, through writing prompts and tools. I consider it a guidebook for transformation through self-expression. My hope is that it will spark creative thought and offer a space for self-reflection—helping my readers to overcome challenges and move forward, just like I did.

I'd love to hear what creative projects you work on to keep yourselves going. I love hearing your stories and experiences and connecting with you.

You can reach me on Facebook and my website at tyramanning.com.

# SELECTED TITLES FROM SHE WRITES PRESS

She Writes Press is an independent publishing company founded to serve women writers everywhere. Visit us at www.shewritespress.com.

*Journey of Memoir: The Three Stages of Memoir Writing* by Linda Joy Myers. $22.95, 978-1-938314-26-1. A straightforward, highly effective workbook designed to help memoirists of every level get their story on the page.

*The Magic of Memoir: Inspiration for Your Writing Journey* by Linda Joy Myers and Brooke Warner. $17.95, 978-1-63152-147-8. Food for the journey and comfort for the soul for memoirists who find themselves in the thick of it, offering interviews with best-selling memoirists and contributions from writers who've gone the distance.

*This Way Up: Seven Tools for Unleashing Your Creative Self and Transforming Your Life* by Patti Clark. $16.95, 978-1-63152-028-0. A story of healing for women who yearn to lead a fuller life, accompanied by a workbook designed to help readers work through personal challenges, discover new inspiration, and harness their creative power.

*What's Your Book? A Step-by-Step Guide to Get You from Inspiration to Published Author* by Brooke Warner. $12.95, 978-1-938314-00-1. An aspiring author's go-to guide for getting from idea to publication.

*Note to Self: A Seven-Step Path to Gratitude and Growth* by Laurie Buchanan. $16.95, 978-1-63152-113-3. Transforming intention into action, *Note to Self* equips you to shed your baggage, bridging the gap between where you are and where you want to be—body, mind, and spirit—and empowering you to step into joy-filled living *now!*

*The Art of Play: Igniting Your Imagination to Unlock Insight, Healing, and Joy* by Joan Stanford. $19.95, 978-1-63152-030-3. Lifelong "non-artist" Joan Stanford shares the creative process that led her to insight and healing, and shares ways for others to do the same.